English for International Tourism

Iwonna Dubicka & Margaret O'Keeffe

Pearson Education Limited
Edinburgh Gate
Harlow
Essex CM20 2JE
England
and Associated Companies throughout the world.

www.longman.com

First published 2003
Sixth impression 2006

ISBN-13: 978-0-582-47988-3
ISBN-10: 0-582-47988-6

Set in Syntax 11 / 15pt

Printed in China   GCC/06

Author acknowledgements

We would like to thank the following people for their contribu-
tions, encouragement and hard work: Darina Farrell, David
Torra, Eustasio Gavilan, Eli Ridler, Albert Prades, Kim
Ashmore, Anne-Marie Hennessy, Anita Herron, Marta La
Torre, Nathalie Lebris, Maribel Marciá, Sean McGuinness,
Jane and Simon Munn, Kelly and Leta O'Donnell, Joan Offroy,
Kash Sandhu, Alison Wilson as well as our friends, families
and students. We would also like to thank Ian Wood, our
editor, for his invaluable input and professionalism and
Diane Legrande at the DK picture library for all her hard work.

The authors and publishers would like to thank the following
people for their help in piloting and developing this course:
Jane Peignard; Noreen Noonan, CRET, Briançon, France;
Graham Stanley, Sant Ignasi-Sarrià, Escola Superior
d'Hosteleria i Turisme, Barcelona, Spain; Joanna
Szerszunowicz, Studium Hotelarstwa i Obsugi Turystyki,
Biaystok, Poland; Boena Wierciska, Wysza Szkoa
Hotelarstwa Gastronomii i Turystyki, Warszawa, Poland.

We are grateful to the following for permission to reproduce
copyright material:

HSA International for extracts from their website
www.hsa.com; Pearson Education Limited for an extract from
Tourism: Principles and Practice by Chris Cooper, John
Fletcher, Stephen Wanhill, David Gilbert and Rebecca
Shepherd; Travelpage.com for an extract from their website
www.cruiseserver.net; and company information from
BA In-Flight Retail, Inghams Travel and P&O Cruises.

Photo acknowledgements

The publishers are grateful to the following for their permission
to reproduce copyright photographs:

Alamo for page 16; AMS Hotel Group, Netherlands for page
32; Art Directors and TRIP for pages 70 and 103 bottom right;
Britania Airways for page 58; British Airways for pages 59, 62
and 63; Corbis Images for pages 52, 53 right, 66 right and
101; DACS for 28 top right; Darina Farrell for page 8 top right;
David Torra, page 62; Empics for page 27 left and top; Greg
Evans International for pages 40 bottom left and 117; Eye
Ubiquitous for pages 8 top and 103 bottom left; Fiordland
Travel for pages 74 top and bottom and 77; Robert Harding
for pages 12 left, 40 right, 53 left, 86 right and 113; Holiday
Inn Crowne Plaza Hotel for page 46 top middle; Image State
for pages 64 left and 98; Inghams Travel for pages 80 and 84;
Philip Lamble for pages 24 left, 28 left, 28 middle, 28 bottom
right and 29 right; Life File Photographic Library for page 103
top left; Link Picture Library for page 46 top right; The
Moviestore Collection for page 100 left; NASA for page 12
right; Richard Nowitz for page 53 bottom right; PA Photos for
page 64 top right; P&O Cruises for page 40 top, 41 top left
and centre, 42, 114 and 116; The Photographers Library for
page 92; Pictor International for page 40 top left; Pictures
Colour Library for page 64 bottom right; Popperfoto for page
82; The Swiss Hotel Management Service for pages 7 and
83; Mark Edward Smith for page 34 bottom left; Travel Ink for
page 10; Up Up and Away Ballooning for page 78 middle right
and Whale Watch, New Zealand for page 78 middle left.

Images taken from DK Eyewitness Travel Guides published by
Dorling Kindersley Limited:

Travel Guide Amsterdam – page 33; Travel Guide Bali and
Lombok – page 78cra; Travel Guide Barcelona – page 24tr,
24c, 25; Travel Guide Berlin – page 11cr; Travel Guide Cracow
– page 66cla, 66cra, 67; Travel Guide Florence and Tuscany –
page 113; Travel Guide Florida – page 12tl, 12c Universal
Studios, 14; Travel Guide Istanbul – page 54cl, 54bl, 54br, 55;
Travel Guide London – page 18tc; Travel Guide Mexico – page
99, 100tc; Travel Guide New York – page 11cl, 18ca, 64cb;
Travel Guide New Zealand – page 75, Travel Guide Paris –
page 11cl; Travel Guide Rome – page 11cl; Travel Guide
Seville and Andalusia – page 11c; Travel Guide South Africa –
page 46tl, 46cra, 49, 78cla; Travel Guide Spain – page 24cr,
28ca, 29ca; Travel Guide St Petersburg – page 11cr; Travel
Guide Thailand – page 18cra, 86tc, 86c, 87cla, 87c, 87cr, 88,
90crb, 91clb, 100tr, 100cl; Travel Guide Venice & Veneto – page
18tl, 18cla, 30tc, 30cl, 30tr, 35cb, 38t, 39ca, 115cb.

We regret that we have been unable to trace the copyright
holders of the photographs on pages 37 and 78 middle far
left and would welcome any information enabling us to do so.

The front cover photographs are all © DK with the exception of
the middle image which is © Quadrant Picture Library/The
Flight Collection. The back cover photographs are all © DK.

Illustrated by:
Jacey, Micky Finn, Jane Spencer, Bill Donohoe and
Peter Greenwood.

English for International Tourism Pre-intermediate

In the hotel and tourism industries English language skills are both a daily requirement and essential for career advancement. In order to function professionally in English, students need not only an understanding of the language system but also an awareness of how to implement it effectively and appropriately. To this end, *English for International Tourism* is a skills-based course supported by a comprehensive language syllabus.

Skills

We have provided lots of tips and guidance to help students develop the essential skills to work in tourism. The hotel and tourism industries are very customer-focused so effective listening and speaking skills are of the utmost importance. Therefore we have provided a wide range of communicative practice, from simple customer service encounters such as hiring a car to preparing and giving mini-presentations. Pronunciation activities not only help students with sounds that are difficult for pre-intermediate learners but also develop professional skills such as showing enthusiasm and politeness.

We have carefully chosen a wide variety of industry-specific contexts and speakers for listening practice: tour guides, travel agents, receptionists, housekeepers and cruise staff, in addition to a variety of native and foreign speakers of English.

Reading and writing activities concentrate on essential tasks such as confirming changes to reservations, describing conference facilities and writing letters of apology. The writing bank at the back of the book gives models and guidelines for writing letters, faxes, emails and CVs.

Language focus

We realise that the basis for speaking a foreign language with confidence is an understanding of its structural system. Therefore we have integrated a comprehensive language syllabus specific to the communicative needs of your students. Grammar is always presented in context and extensively practised. Functional language is also presented in context and then highlighted in professional practice boxes that provide useful frameworks for key customer service encounters such as telephone bookings, giving advice and dealing with problems.

As the book is designed for vocational students, we felt it especially important to develop industry-related vocabulary, ranging from hotel duties and facilities to cruise ships and ecotourism. We have also recycled and extended this vocabulary in the consolidation units and workbook.

Authentic materials

We have created realistic tasks based on a variety of authentic texts to give students first-hand experience of webpages, job advertisements, hotel bills, customer service questionnaires, menus and entertainment programmes. We have also integrated extracts from Dorling Kindersley's *Eyewitness Travel Guides* because they are visually attractive, relevant and motivating for learners. These sections typify the key information travel guides offer such as maps, sightseeing tips, getting around, accommodation and cultural advice so that your students are given an insight into different countries and cultures.

Internet

As the hotel and tourism industries are at the forefront of the e-commerce and e-business revolution we felt the internet should be an integral part of any tourism course. The web tasks we suggest will encourage your students to engage with tourism-related websites and can be done either in class or as self-study. You can also use these web tasks as a basis for project work.

Revision and consolidation

The three coursebook consolidation units help learners review language and specific vocabulary as well as offering extra skills practice. Furthermore, there is also a workbook and teacher's book to accompany the coursebook.

The self-study workbook provides extra skills, grammar and vocabulary practice. In the teacher's book you will find lesson plans, extra teaching ideas, photocopiable materials and tourism information about the countries and cities featured in the coursebook.

We hope you enjoy using *English for International Tourism*.

Iwonna Dubicka
Margaret O'Keeffe

English for International Tourism Pre-intermediate

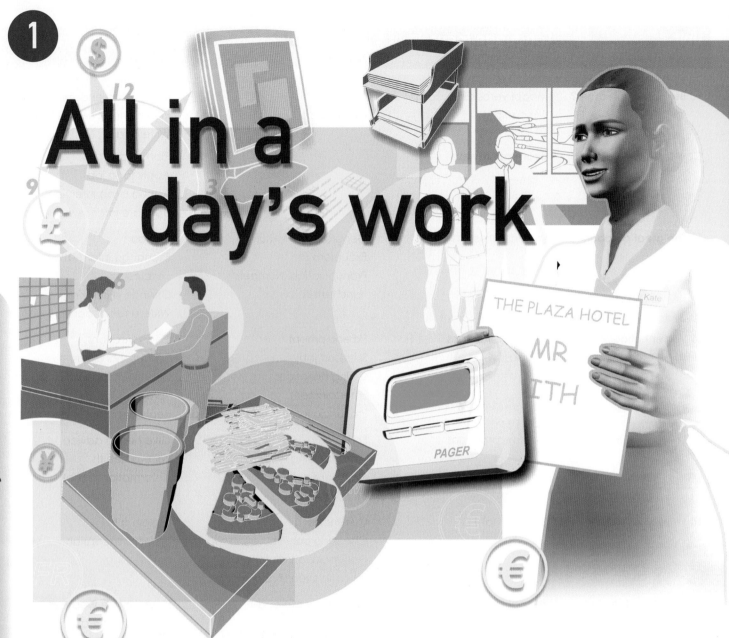

All in a day's work

speaking **1 Look at the picture. What are the advantages and disadvantages of working in a hotel? Compare your answers with your partner's.**

reading **2 Where do you think the article on the opposite page is taken from?**

a) a newspaper

b) a careers guide

c) a hotel brochure

3 Read the article again and answer these questions.

1 Find five jobs or areas of work that are mentioned in the text.

2 Why is the hospitality industry not always hospitable?

3 What responsibilities does a hotel manager have in a small hotel?

4 In what ways is the hospitality industry different from other industries?

5 Find three adjectives that describe a career in the hospitality industry.

Underline or highlight the part of the text where you found your answers.

Not always hospitable

Hospitality may be one of the most exciting industries to work in but as Asha Khan reports, it isn't an easy life.

The hospitality industry is one of the fastest-growing industries in the world. It offers some exciting careers and a lot of job satisfaction. But it isn't easy working in a hotel – the peak holiday season is hard work, with employees often working long hours and sometimes seven days a week.

Teamwork

Every member of staff, from the housekeeper to the hotel manager, is responsible for the hotel. In smaller hotels and motels one manager is usually responsible for rooms, the food and beverage service, registration and general management. There is a wide variety of jobs in larger hotels, including administration jobs such as accountant and marketing executive.

Benefits

Hotel employees get paid sick leave and holidays, as well as other benefits like free food and, occasionally, free holidays! Many hotels also offer free or cheap live-in accommodation and have resident managers and concierges.

People

The hospitality industry is different from other industries. Hospitality is people dealing with people, from the porter to the hotel manager. If you don't like people, this isn't the career for you.

vocabulary **Hotel jobs**

4 Match the jobs with the duties. Use a dictionary to help you.

1 chambermaid	a) carries guests' bags to their rooms
2 hotel manager	b) cleans guestrooms
3 bartender	c) serves guests in the restaurant
4 accountant	d) manages all the hotel staff
5 concierge	e) serves guests at the bar
6 porter	f) finds business for the hotel
7 waiter	g) gives information and helps guests
8 marketing manager	h) does the hotel's finances

pronunciation **The /h/ sound**

5 Which word does not have the /h/ sound? Practise saying the words.

| hotel | hospitality | holiday | hours | housekeeper | happy | help |

speaking **6 Work in pairs. What do you like about the hospitality industry? Write down five things and then compare your ideas with your partner's.**

listening **Daily duties**

7 Darina Farrell is the Assistant Housekeeper in the Bahama Beach Hotel in the Caribbean. Listen and answer the questions.

1 What are SOs?

2 What are COs?

8 What do the housekeepers usually do if they have an SO? Listen again and tick (✓) the phrases you hear.

a) change the sheets ✓   e) clean the bathroom

b) use the computer   f) make the bed

c) check the soap   g) tidy the bedroom

d) change the towels   h) use air freshener

9 Darina talks about her working hours. Listen and answer the questions.

1 How many days a week does she work?

2 How often does she work at the weekend?

3 When does she have some free time?

4 What hours does she sometimes work on Mondays?

Language focus Adverbs of frequency

Look at the examples and underline the correct option below.

*Darina **always** works on Saturdays and Sundays.*
*She **usually** works from nine to one.*
*The hotel isn't **often** busy on Tuesdays.*
*They **sometimes** work until three in the afternoon.*
*Darina **hardly ever** finishes early on Mondays.*
*She is **never** late for work.*

We put the adverbs *always, usually, often, sometimes, hardly ever* and *never* before / after the verb *be* and before / after other verbs.

▶ For more information turn to page 125.

speaking **10** Work in pairs. Write six sentences about your partner, using *always, usually, often, sometimes, hardly ever* **and** *never*.

listening

11 Listen to Darina and complete the notes.

1 She's responsible for ....six.......... to .... chambermaids.
2 One of her main duties is to .... new staff.
3 She has a bleeper so that people .... her.
4 After the chambermaids have cleaned the rooms, she .... that everything is OK.

Language focus Present simple

- We use the present simple for regular activities and situations.
- We make negative sentences and questions with *do / does*.

  New chambermaids **don't work** *alone.*
  Why **does** *she* **carry** *a bleeper?*

- With *she, he, it* we put *-s* at the end of verbs.
  cleans, trains, likes, plays, goes, flies

▶ For more information turn to page 125.

---

practice

12 Complete the interview with the correct form of the verbs in brackets.

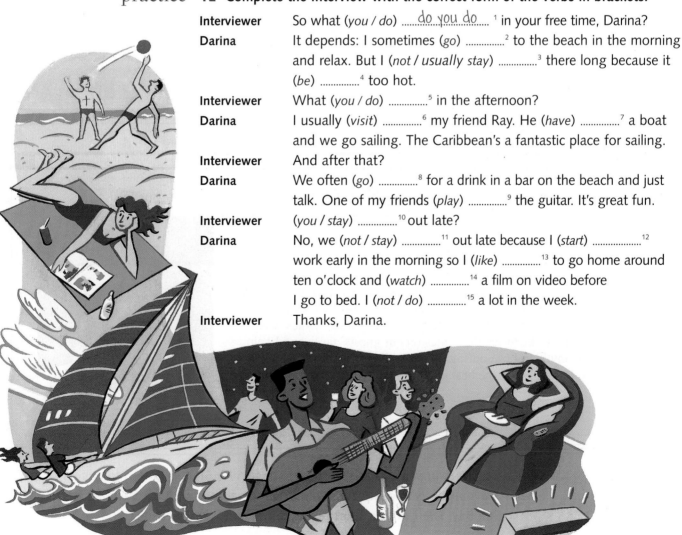

Interviewer	So what (*you / do*) .....do you do..... ¹ in your free time, Darina?
Darina	It depends: I sometimes (*go*) ....² to the beach in the morning and relax. But I (*not / usually stay*) ....³ there long because it (*be*) ....⁴ too hot.
Interviewer	What (*you / do*) ....⁵ in the afternoon?
Darina	I usually (*visit*) ....⁶ my friend Ray. He (*have*) ....⁷ a boat and we go sailing. The Caribbean's a fantastic place for sailing.
Interviewer	And after that?
Darina	We often (*go*) ....⁸ for a drink in a bar on the beach and just talk. One of my friends (*play*) ....⁹ the guitar. It's great fun.
Interviewer	(*you / stay*) ....¹⁰ out late?
Darina	No, we (*not / stay*) ....¹¹ out late because I (*start*) ....¹² work early in the morning so I (*like*) ....¹³ to go home around ten o'clock and (*watch*) ....¹⁴ a film on video before I go to bed. I (*not / do*) ....¹⁵ a lot in the week.
Interviewer	Thanks, Darina.

13 Work in groups of three. Discuss these topics and complete the sentences below.

| family | free time | travel | study | work | favourite holiday destinations |

All of us …   Two of us …   One of us …   None of us …

The /s/, /z/ and /ɪz/ sounds

14 What is the pronunciation of the letter *s* at the end of these words? Put them in the correct groups.

| goes | watches | flies | starts | washes | wants | finishes | arrives |

/s/	/z/	/ɪz/
likes	plays	changes

15 Read the webpage below. Are these statements true or false? Correct any false statements.

1 Vanessa hasn't worked at the hotel for very long.
2 She's very happy with her job.
3 She always tries to use guests' names.
4 She does the same things every day.

Address: http://www.sunbay.com/staffprofile.html

SUN BAY HOTEL – MEET OUR STAFF.

Vanessa Perez
Reception / Front Desk

I've been here at the Sun Bay Hotel since it opened. I am proud to be part of such a great team of people and look forward to being here for many years to come. I always try to remember guests' names when they get here. I like to see the smiles on our guests' faces and I help them with anything I can during their stay. Every day is different at the hotel. I think I have the best job in town.

16 Work in pairs. Student A turn to page 113. Student B turn to page 117. Ask questions to complete the information about two staff members at the Sun Bay. Then write a short text about them for the website.

vocabulary **Nationalities**

17 Match the countries with the pictures. Then write the nationality for each country.

| USA ǀ | France | Spain | Italy | Russia | Germany |

speaking **18** Work in pairs. Student A turn to page 114. Student B look at the information below and ask your partner questions to complete the Sun Bay Hotel register.

What's the name of the guest in room 212?   Can you spell that for me?
Where's he / she from? What's his / her passport number?

Room	Name	Nationality	Passport number
211	Mrs Andropov	Russian	4915564GA
212	Mr Brandt	....	....
308	Ms Winger	American	B591247900
319	....	....	....
415	Mr Cervantes	Spanish	X1671621V
417	....	....	....
502	Mr Xiao	Chinese	Q709867403
507	....	....	....

Fly-drive holidays

speaking

1 Match the pictures with the places in the box.

Disney World Theme Park 4   Kennedy Space Center
Universal Studios   Daytona Beach

listening

2 A travel agent deals with a telephone enquiry about Florida. In what order do you think the following will be mentioned? Listen and check your answers.

- ☐ a) total price of the holiday
- ☐ b) dates of the flights
- ☐ c) names of the people travelling
- ☐ d) type of accommodation
- ☐ e) method of payment
- ☐ f) destination

3 Listen again and answer these questions.

1 What three things are included in a fly-drive holiday?
2 What types of accommodation are available?
3 When does the guest want to travel?
4 What do the numbers 14 and 543 refer to?
5 How often are the flights to Florida?
6 Which airport do the flights to Florida go from?

Special offers ✳

US fly-drive holidays
Florida 7 nts and
14 nts from £399
Tel. World Breaks
020 7946 0004

4 Listen again and complete the reservation form below.

SELLING A HOLIDAY

- Be informative.
- Imagine it is your holiday.
- Be friendly.
- Sound enthusiastic.

☀ **World Breaks**	**Reservations**
Type of holiday:	US fly-drive
Resort name:	Orlando
Type of accommodation:	 1
Number of nights:	 2
Out date:	 3
Departure airport:	LHR
Return date:	 4
Departure airport:	ORL
Number of adults:	 5
Name(s):	 6
Number of children:	 7
Name(s):	 8

Professional practice Telephone enquiries

The following phrases are useful when answering the telephone.

- introduce yourself and offer to be of assistance
  Good afternoon, World Breaks, Janet Cookson speaking.
  How can I help you?

- be enthusiastic
  That's a very good time to go.
  We have a great offer at the moment.

- make sure you get all the necessary information
  Can I have the names of the people travelling, please?
  Could you spell your surname for me, please?

- check the information
  Just let me confirm the details.
  Is that correct?

speaking **5 Work in pairs. Student A turn to page 113. You are a travel agent. Student B, you saw an advertisement for the fly-drive deals to Tuscany. Phone the travel agent and ask about dates, accommodation and price.**

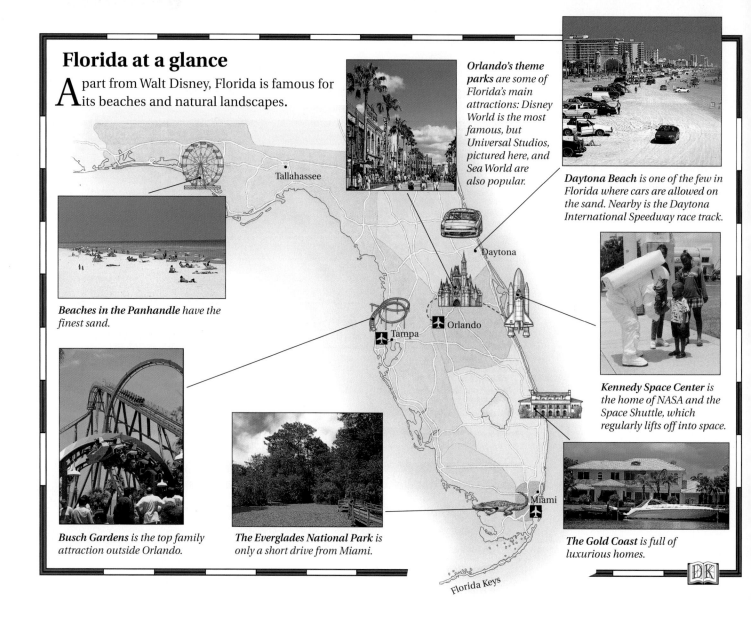

Florida at a glance

Apart from Walt Disney, Florida is famous for its beaches and natural landscapes.

Orlando's theme parks are some of Florida's main attractions: Disney World is the most famous, but Universal Studios, pictured here, and Sea World are also popular.

Daytona Beach is one of the few in Florida where cars are allowed on the sand. Nearby is the Daytona International Speedway race track.

Beaches in the Panhandle have the finest sand.

Kennedy Space Center is the home of NASA and the Space Shuttle, which regularly lifts off into space.

Busch Gardens is the top family attraction outside Orlando.

The Everglades National Park is only a short drive from Miami.

The Gold Coast is full of luxurious homes.

Tallahassee
Daytona
Orlando
Tampa
Miami
Florida Keys

DK

reading

6 Look at the map and photos of Florida and answer these questions.

1 Name four theme parks in Florida.
2 Where are Florida's best beaches?
3 Where is the space museum?
4 Where can you see motor racing?
5 Where can you see areas of natural beauty?
6 In which part of Florida do a lot of rich people live?
7 Where can you see movie stars?

7 Oscar is going on holiday to Florida. Look at the email to his friend Jackie on the opposite page and answer these questions.

1 How long is Oscar staying in Florida?
2 Where is he flying to?
3 When is he arriving in Florida?
4 What time is he arriving?
5 Where would he like to meet Jackie?

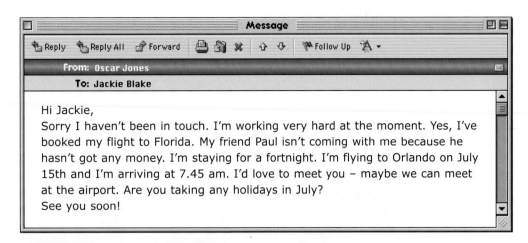

> *From:* Oscar Jones
> *To:* Jackie Blake

Hi Jackie,

Sorry I haven't been in touch. I'm working very hard at the moment. Yes, I've booked my flight to Florida. My friend Paul isn't coming with me because he hasn't got any money. I'm staying for a fortnight. I'm flying to Orlando on July 15th and I'm arriving at 7.45 am. I'd love to meet you – maybe we can meet at the airport. Are you taking any holidays in July?

See you soon!

listening

8 Listen to Oscar phone Jackie. Draw the rest of his itinerary on the map of Florida and then answer these questions.

1 Why does Jackie sound tired?
2 How is Oscar travelling around Florida?
3 Why can't Jackie go to Disney World with Oscar?
4 What is Oscar doing the first weekend of his holiday?
5 What is he doing at the end of the holiday?
6 Is he meeting Jackie?

Language focus **Present continuous**

- We use the present continuous for current or temporary activities.
  I'**m working** very hard at the moment.

- We also use the present continuous for future arrangements.
  Are you **taking** any holidays in July?

  My friend Paul **isn't coming** with me.

- Some verbs are not used in the present continuous.
  Jane **knows** a good travel agent.
  Mr Craig **wants** to go to Miami.

▶ For more information turn to pages 125 and 131.

speaking

9 Plan a holiday from the information below. Then ask other students about their holiday plans. Who might you meet in Florida and where?

Dates	Airport	Sights
28 June – 12 July	Miami	Orlando's Theme Parks
12 July – 26 July	Orlando	Kennedy Space Center
26 July – 9 August	Tampa	Everglades National Park

webtask

10 Find information about Florida on the internet or in travel guides and plan a one-week holiday for yourself and friends.

speaking   Car hire

11 Which of these cars is most suitable for a family of four travelling in Florida? Why?

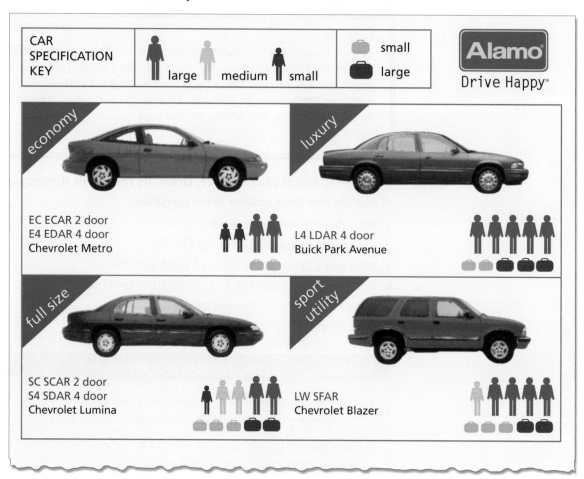

vocabulary   **12 Match the phrases with their definitions.**

1 seven-day rental   a) place where you collect the car
2 air conditioning   b) car hire for one week only
3 collision damage waiver (CDW)   c) in-car temperature control
4 an additional charge   d) insurance cover for the driver
5 third-party liability   e) an extra cost
6 a pick-up location   f) insurance cover for other road users

listening   **13 A car hire agent deals with a telephone enquiry. Listen and put his actions in the correct order.**

| 1 | a) asks for the caller's name
| | b) asks for the pick-up date
| | c) confirms the car group
| | d) explains what ALI means
| | e) recommends additional insurance
| | f) confirms the price

Do you think the car hire agent was helpful? Why / why not?

pronunciation **Politeness**

14 **Listen to the stressed words in these sentences. Then practise saying the sentences politely.**

1 How can I <u>help you</u>?

2 <u>Can</u> I <u>have</u> your <u>name</u>, please, <u>sir</u>?

3 <u>Just</u> one <u>moment</u>, sir.

4 <u>Sorry</u>, could you <u>repeat</u> that, <u>please</u>?

5 <u>Thank</u> you for <u>calling</u>!

Professional practice   Making calls

The following phrases are useful when making calls.

• identify yourself when you phone
Hello, this is Janet Cookson from World Breaks.

• ask for the person you want to speak to
Could you put me through to Gabriella, please?

• explain why you are calling
I'm calling about the holiday on page 84 of your brochure.

• if you leave a message, leave your name and number
Please call Janet Cookson on 020 946 0008.

---

speaking **15** **Work in pairs. Student B, turn to page 115. Student A, you work for World Breaks car hire, Miami. Answer the phone and complete the reservation screen below.**

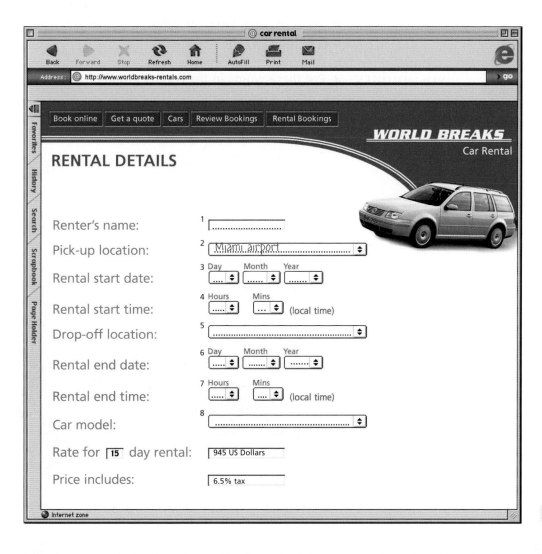

Table for two

speaking   **1** Match the dishes with the pictures.

Phanaeng curry 3   roast beef   banana split   spaghetti   seafood

2 Work in pairs. Find out what your partner's favourite meal is and what sort of food he/she never eats.

vocabulary   **3** Put these words in the correct groups. Use a dictionary to help you.

salmon   banana   chicken   tuna   orange   beef
cod   peas   apple   potatoes   carrots   lamb

Fish	Meat	Vegetables	Fruit
salmon			

Now add more words to each list.

4 Match these words with the pictures. Use a dictionary to help you.

fry 3   stuff   roast   boil   grill   bake

How can you cook the food in exercise 3?

reading

5 Look at the two menus. Where do you think they come from?

a) a pizzeria

b) a business-class flight

c) a British pub

d) a fast-food restaurant

1

Hungarian goulash with rice

Spaghetti carbonara

Cod, chips and peas

Roast lamb with roast potatoes, peas and carrots

Chicken curry and rice

Cheeseburger, chips and salad

Vegetarian terrine made with goat's cheese and aubergines

Range of sandwiches and salads

Please pay for your food when you order at the bar

2 Menu

Appetisers

Main course

Chicken stuffed with ricotta cheese served with ratatouille

Salmon and tuna bake served with béchamel sauce

Dessert

White chocolate mousse with orange segments

A range of wines, minerals and spirits are available from the bar

vocabulary **Describing food**

6 Match the verbs with the phrases. Use a dictionary to help you.

1 made with   a) cook in an oven without using oil or fat

2 range of   b) list of ingredients in a dish

3 stuff with   c) accompanies a main dish

4 roast   d) fill with something

5 bake   e) cook in oil or fat in an oven or over a fire

6 served with   f) number of similar things

7 Match the dishes with the ingredients.

1 Hungarian goulash is made with   a) a mayonnaise dressing.

2 Ratatouille is made with   b) beef and vegetables.

3 Ratafia is made from   c) almonds.

4 Pasta is made from   d) tomatoes and lettuce.

5 A seafood cocktail is served with   e) flour, eggs and water.

6 Hamburgers are often served with   f) red peppers, aubergines and courgettes.

8 Look at the menus again. What would you order to eat in each place?

Language focus Countable and uncountable nouns

Look at the examples and underline the correct options below.

*I'd like **a cheeseburger**, please.*
*Would you like **rice** with that?*

- Countable nouns have a singular or plural form. You *can / cannot* count them.
- Uncountable nouns only have a singular form. You *can / cannot* count them.
- You *can / cannot* use *a* or *an* before an uncountable noun.

▶ For more information turn to page 126.

9 Put these words in the correct groups. Use a dictionary to help you.

chocolate broccoli potato rice coffee juice aubergine omelette
salmon milk sugar salt prawn fruit chicken sandwich lettuce
pizza spaghetti salad meal food tomato curry vegetable

countable	both	uncountable
meal	chocolate	broccoli

pronunciation **Word stress**

10 Now listen to the words and put them in the correct groups below according to their stress pattern.

■	■ ▪	■ ▪ ▪	▪ ■ ▪
rice	coffee	broccoli	potato

Language focus *Some* and *any*

Look at the examples and complete the information below with *some* or *any*.

*She made **some sandwiches**.*   *He never eats **any vegetables**.*
*Can I have **some juice**?*   *There isn't **any bread**.*
*Would you like **some fruit**?*   *Did you buy **any milk**?*

- We use .some. in positive sentences and with offers and requests.
- We use .... in negative sentences and questions.
- We use both .... and .... with plural countable nouns and uncountable nouns.

▶ For more information turn to page 126.

practice   **11 Complete the sentences with** *a / an*, *some* **or** *any*.

1 Would you like .....some.... more wine, sir?
2 She doesn't want .... glass of wine.
3 Could I have .... salt, please?
4 Are there .... tables free?
5 We've got .... orange juice but we haven't got .... tomato juice.
6 She doesn't like .... kind of cheese.
7 Could I have .... clean knife, please?
8 Can I have .... fried egg and .... bacon for breakfast?

vocabulary   **Recording vocabulary**

12 Work in pairs. Look at the following tips for recording vocabulary. Which do you think are the most useful?

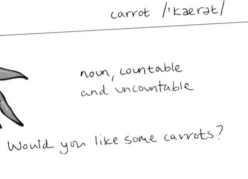

carrot /ˈkaerət/

noun, countable
and uncountable

Would you like some carrots?

fish /fɪʃ/

noun, countable and uncountable
How much fish would you like?
How many fish did you catch?

1 Buy a good dictionary, such as the *Longman WordWise Dictionary*, that shows the pronunciation and the part of speech (noun, verb, adjective, adverb).
2 Always remember to write down useful words. Use small cards, lists and diagrams to help you.
3 Write down the part of speech and check the pronunciation, including the word stress pattern, of any new words in your dictionary.
4 Draw a picture, write a definition or an example sentence to help you remember it.
5. It's a good idea to revise new words late at night or first thing in the morning – use your cards, lists and diagrams to help you.

13 Use a dictionary to find out information about the following words.

| mousse | reserve | deduct | mayonnaise | bill |

mousse /muːs/ *n* [C,U] **1** a sweet food made from a mixture of cream, eggs and fruit or chocolate which is eaten when it is cold: *chocolate mousse* **2** a white slightly sticky substance that you put in your hair to make it look thicker or to hold it in place

14 Think of a traditional dish served in your country. Write a list of ingredients and say how it is served.

Language focus *Much, many, a lot (of)*

Look at the sentences and complete the information with *much, many* or *a lot (of)*.

*She doesn't eat **much** fruit.*
*How **much** coffee do you drink a day?*
*I didn't eat **many** cakes at the party.*

*How **many** sandwiches did you make?*
*You've made **a lot of** cheese sandwiches.*
*He always puts **a lot of** salt on his food.*

- We use ...much... in questions and negative sentences with uncountable nouns.
- We use .... in questions and negative sentences with countable nouns.
- We use .... in positive sentences with both countable and uncountable nouns.

▶ For more information turn to page 126.

practice

15 Complete the dialogue with *much, many* or *a lot (of)*.

Carlo   I'll try the *mole poblano* – it's a speciality of the house.

Luisa   The menu says it's turkey covered in a chilli and chocolate sauce!

Carlo   That's right. They use ......a lot of......[1] chocolate and spicy sauces in Mexican cooking.

Luisa   I'll have something else. I don't eat ....[2] meat these days and there aren't ....[3] fish dishes here.

Carlo   Yes, but they eat ....[4] beans in Mexico. Why don't you have some refried beans and guacamole with tortillas?

Luisa   How ....[5] tortillas do I get?

Carlo   If you don't want ....[6] to eat, why not start with three or four?

Luisa   You're right! I want to have a dessert too. I see there are ....[7] exotic fruits like watermelons and papaya to choose from.

listening

16 Listen to three conversations in a restaurant. What are the guests complaining about in each situation?

17 Listen again. Are these statements true or false? Correct any false statements.

1 The first guest thinks there is a mistake on the bill.
2 The first guest had two bottles of water.
3 The cashier made a mistake.
4 Some of the group of twelve are late.
5 The waiter has served the drinks to the group.
6 The third guest complains the food is too cold.
7 The waiter returns with an overdone steak.

Professional practice Dealing with complaints

The following phrases are useful when dealing with complaints.

- apologise
  I'm very sorry, sir / madam.

- give a reason for the problem
  I thought you ordered two bottles of water.
  There's been a mistake.

- promise to take action (*I'll ...*)
  I'll deal with it right away.

vocabulary Complaining about food

18 Match the complaints with the pictures.

a) It's too hot. 2

b) It's too cold.

c) They are overdone.

d) The service is too slow.

e) It's too expensive.

Language focus Complaining about food

The following phrases are useful when complaining about food.

- *too + adjective*
  It's **too hot**.

- *not + adjective + enough*
  This water is**n't cold enough**.

- *there + be not + enough + noun*
  There isn't enough ice.

- *over / under + past participle*
  This steak is **undercooked**.

---

speaking 19 Work in pairs. Student A, you are a guest at the Metropolis restaurant. Student B, you are a waiter. Look at the pictures again and role-play the conversations. Use some of these phrases.

I'm very sorry, sir / madam.	There's been a mistake.
I'll check the bill.	I'll deal with it right away.
We'll deduct it from the bill.	I'll bring another one straightaway.
I'll be with you in a minute.	I'll ask the chef to heat it up.

City tours

Harbour café ▶

▲ Barcelona bus tour

▲ Barcelona Football Club

▲ Sitges beach

City tours – Barcelona

speaking

1 Look at the tourist attractions in Barcelona. Which of them would be of interest to these tourists?

a young married couple	a group of students
a family with young children	a married couple in their 50s

2 Work in pairs. Which of these attractions would interest your partner? Why?

reading

3 Read the article on the opposite page. Which is the best title for it?

1 The life of Antoni Gaudí
2 The making of the *Sagrada Familia*
3 Famous sights of Barcelona

4 Read the article again and answer these questions.

1 Which four works by Gaudí are mentioned in the article?
2 What works did Gaudí produce after 1909?
3 What hours did Gaudí work?
4 Why didn't taxi drivers take him to hospital after his accident?
5 What was Gaudí's philosophy when he designed his works?

BARCELONA'S MOST famous architect, Antoni Gaudí, was born in 1852. The city is full of his work, including the many houses he built for rich industrialists, like the famous *La Pedrera* (*Casa Milà*) building and *Palacio Güell.*

From 1909 until 1926 Gaudí worked only on the *Sagrada Familia* (pictured below). He got up at seven o'clock in the morning every day and walked to mass in Gracia. He ate lunch in his workshop and worked until six or seven in the evening. He often didn't eat for long periods of time. His furniture was an old bed and an uncomfortable sofa and he had an old coat for a blanket.

Dragon covered with brightly coloured tiles, guarding the steps in the Parc Güell.

In 1890 the industrialist Eusebi Güell commissioned Gaudí to design a park on a hill above the city. Gaudí worked on *Parc Güell* for the next fourteen years. He hated straight lines and wanted to show nature in all his works, like the curved shapes in stones, waves and wet sand.

On the evening of 7 June 1926 a tram hit him as he tried to cross a road. He was dirty and wearing old clothes. No one recognised him. Taxi drivers refused to take him to hospital. Eventually, someone took him to a public hospital. When they discovered who he was, they moved him to a private room. He died three days later. His church is still unfinished but modern architects are continuing the work today.

STAR FEATURES
★ Passion Façade
★ Nativity Façade
★ Crypt

★ Nativity Façade

★ Crypt

★ Passion Façade

Main entrance

5 Why are these dates important in the Gaudí story?

1852   1909   1890–1904   7 June 1926   10 June 1926

speaking **6 Think of a famous architect from your country. What buildings did he / she design?**

Language focus Past simple

- We use the past simple to talk about events and actions that are finished.
  *He **died** three days later.*
- We form the past simple of regular verbs by adding -ed.
  *He **worked** until six or seven in the evening.*
- Irregular verbs (see page 131) have a different form in the past.
  *He also **built** many houses for rich industrialists in the city.*

  Find five regular and five irregular past simple forms in the text on page 25.

- We form the negative of the past simple tense with *didn't* + the infinitive.
  *Gaudí often **didn't eat** for long periods of time.*
- We form questions with *did* + subject + the infinitive.
  ***Did** Gaudí **live** in Barcelona?*

▶ For more information turn to page 126.

pronunciation   **-ed endings**

7 Put these words in the correct groups according to the pronunciation of the -ed endings.

worked   moved   hated   walked   refused   wanted
discovered   needed   finished   lived   opened

/t/	/d/	/ɪd/
worked	moved	hated

practice   **8 Put the verbs in brackets in the correct form.**

1 Picasso's family (*move*) .....moved..... to Barcelona in 1895.

2 (*you / go*) .... to the Picasso Museum when you
  (*be*) .... in Barcelona last month?

3 We (*eat*) .... seafood in a great restaurant in the Olympic Port.

4 Mary (*want*) .... to see all the sights so she
  (*take*) .... the tourist bus around the city.

5 They (*buy*) .... a lot of souvenirs when they
  (*go*) .... shopping in the *Ramblas*.

6 Unfortunately, James (*not have*) .... time to visit Parc Güell
  when he (*be*) .... in Barcelona.

7 I (*ask*) .... the hotel receptionist for a good place to eat.

8 The taxi driver (*not understand*) .... us and
  (*refuse*) .... to take us to our hotel.

9 We (*walk*) .... to the top of *La Pedrera*. The views
  (*be*) .... fantastic from up there.

10 (*you / see*) .... any famous people when you
  (*visit*) .... Barcelona Football Club?

9 Complete the text about Barcelona Football Club with the correct form of the verbs in brackets.

Profile
Barcelona

More than a club

Més que un club is the motto of Barcelona FC: 'More than a club'. It has above all, however, been a symbol of Catalan pride.

FC Barcelona (*play*) .....played.....[1] its first ever match on 8 December 1899. They (*lose*) ....[2] 0–1 to a team of British citizens who (*live*) ....[3] in Barcelona at the time. The club (*move*) ....[4] several times but (*not / move*) ....[5] to its present stadium until 1957. The club (*need*) ....[6] a new stadium because the old one (*not be*) ....[7] large enough for the number of supporters going to see matches every week. The new stadium (*take*) ....[8] three and a half years to build. On 24 September 1957, FC Barcelona (*have*) ....[9] their first match against Warsaw. Soon, the Barcelona fans (*give*) ....[10] the stadium its popular Catalan nick-name, *Nou Camp*. On the same day, 27 years later, the club's museum (*open*) ....[11]. For the first time, all the club's trophies (*be*) ....[12] in one place. Today, *Nou Camp* is the largest stadium in Europe, with room for 98,000 fans.

21

webtask **Famous buildings**

10 Find information about a famous building on the internet or in a travel guide. Write a short text about the building and present it to your class.

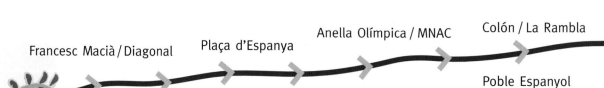

Francesc Macià / Diagonal

Plaça d'Espanya

Anella Olímpica / MNAC

Colón / La Rambla

Poble Espanyol

Passeig de Gràcia / La Pedrera

Estació de Sants

Telefèric de Montjuïc / Fundació Joan Miró

speaking

City bus tour

11 Work in pairs. Think of five difficulties tour guides have at work.

listening

12 Jenny is a bus tour guide in Barcelona. Listen and tick (✔) the difficulties she has.

1 The tourists asked her a lot of questions. ✔
2 She forgot or didn't know some of the information.
3 One of the tourists didn't hear her.
4 The tourists didn't want to pay for the fountain show.
5 A thief stole a woman's handbag.
6 A child wanted to go swimming in the fountains.

▲ A Bus Turístic tour guide

vocabulary

Question words

13 Match these question words with the questions.

Where	When	What	How long	How much	Why	Who

1 _Where_ are the Magic Fountains?
2 .... did the Magic Fountains show first start?
3 .... does the fountain show last?
4 .... does the fountain show cost?
5 .... do the tourists have to be careful?
6 .... time do the tourists have to be back in the bus?
7 .... wants to go swimming in the fountains?

Port Olímpic   Port Vell   Pla de Palau   Barri Gòtic

Vila Olímpica   Parc de la Ciutadella / Zoo

vocabulary **Giving directions**

14 Complete the information from Jenny's tour with words from the box.

> opposite   over there   near   from   in   on   up   straight ahead   in

1 ...On.. your left you can see the sculpture.
2 Our next stop .... Barcelona is the famous Magic Fountains in *Plaça d'Espanya*, that's 'Spain Square', ... the National Palace.
3 Did you say the Olympic stadium is .... here?
4 The sports stadium we visited this afternoon is further .... the hill.
5 You can see the fountains now, ...
6 If you would like to video the show, the best place is .... the footbridge.
7 I'm afraid you can't swim .... the fountains.
8 There is a café ....

15 Look at the tapescript of Jenny's bus tour on page 134. Underline any useful expressions for giving a bus tour.

On your left ...

16 Do you think Jenny gave a good bus tour? Why / why not?

speaking **Guided tours**

17 Work in groups. Prepare a short bus tour for part of your town or city. Use pictures and draw a map of the route. Consider the following points.

- places of interest in the area
- factual information (opening and closing times, prices)
- historical information
- any other interesting facts

18 Listen to the bus tours of the other people in your class and ask questions about the places of interest.

What time does it open / close?   How long does the tour last?
How much does it cost?   Can I ... ?

GUIDED TOURS

When giving a guided tour always remember **PIE**:

- **Politeness**, especially when answering questions.
- Give clear and accurate **information**.
- Show **enthusiasm**.

5

Pensione Do Pozzi ▶

Water cities

▲ Londra Palace

▲ Hotel Marconi

HOTEL MARCONI

speaking   **1** Look at the pictures of hotels in Venice. What do you think their star ratings are? What kind of rooms, facilities and services would you expect to find in these hotels?

listening   **2** Listen to two guests and choose the best hotel for each of them.

Guest 1 ....   Guest 2 ....

vocabulary   **Hotel facilities**

3 Match the words to make hotel facilities and services.

1 en suite   a) dryer
2 24-hour   b) bathroom
3 quality   c) furnishings
4 spacious   d) telephone
5 hair   e) service
6 direct-dial   f) room service
7 satellite   g) cleaning
8 porter   h) rooms
9 dry   i) TV

speaking   **4** What are the most important facilities for you when staying in a hotel?

reading   **5 Read the hotel descriptions and match them to their star ratings.**

| one star³ | two star | three star | four star | five star |

1

A degree of luxury is included at this level. Public areas and bedrooms are more spacious with quality furnishings and décor and satellite TV. The en suite bathrooms are fully equipped. A variety of services is provided, such as porter service, 24-hour room service, laundry and dry-cleaning. Staff will have very good technical and social skills, anticipating and responding to guests' needs.

2

Hotels in this category provide luxury and exceptional comfort. The restaurant has a high level of technical skill, producing dishes to the highest international standards. Staff are well trained in customer care and are especially attentive, efficient and courteous.

3

Hotels in this category offer practical accommodation and are probably small with a family atmosphere. Facilities and meals are simple. Some bedrooms do not have an en suite bath or shower room, although maintenance, cleanliness and comfort need to be of an acceptable standard.

4

In this classification hotels are typically small to medium sized and offer more extensive facilities than at the one-star level. Guests can find more comfortable and well-equipped accommodation, usually with an en suite bath / shower room and colour TV. Hotel staff will offer a more professional service than at the one-star level.

5

Hotels are usually larger and provide a greater quality and range of facilities than at the lower levels. All bedrooms have a complete en suite bath / shower room and offer a better standard of comfort and equipment, such as a direct-dial telephone, a hairdryer and toiletries in the bathroom. Room service is also provided and staff respond well to guests' needs.

6 Read the text again and underline examples of the following.

1 room facilities
2 hotel facilities
3 three adjectives used to describe hotel staff
4 five adjectives used to describe hotels

speaking   **7 What are the best hotels in your city or area? What makes them special?**

8 **Which of these facilities would you expect to find in a two-star hotel?**

> minibar   satellite TV   en suite shower room   bar
> 24-hour room service   laundry service   restaurant

listening **9** **Renee Toonen, owner of the Omega Hotel in Amsterdam, talks about the recent upgrading of the hotel from two to four stars. Number the following in the order that Renee mentions them.**

> 24-hour room service   reception area   fully-equipped bathrooms
> bar   food service   minibar and colour TV |

▲ Omega Hotel, Amsterdam

10 **Listen again and match the two parts of the sentences:**

1 People want	a) a lot more comfortable.
2 The rooms are now	b) a higher standard of accommodation.
3 The furniture is	c) range of food.
4 Bedrooms in two-star hotels are	d) as friendly as before.
5 The reception area has been made	e) bigger.
6 We offer a wider	f) not as spacious as in four-star hotels.
7 We want the atmosphere to be	g) better quality.

Language focus Comparatives and superlatives

Look at the examples in exercise 10 and complete the information below.

In comparative sentences, we put *than* after the adjective. In superlative sentences, we put *the* before the adjective.

- One-syllable adjectives
  - To form the comparative, add ....*-er*.......
  - To form the superlative, add ....
  - When an adjective has a consonant after a vowel, double the final consonant: *big-* '...................' *biggest*.

- Two- and three-syllable adjectives
  - To form the comparative, put .... before the adjective.
  - To form the superlative, put .... before the adjective.

- Two-syllable adjectives ending in -y
  - To form the comparative, change -y to -ier.
  - To form the superlative, change -y to -iest.

- Comparing equals
  - To say two things are equal, use *as* + adjective + *as*.
    *We want the atmosphere to be **as friendly** and informal **as** before.*
  - To make a negative comparison, use *not as* + adjective + *as*.
    *Bedrooms in two-star hotels are **not as spacious as** in four-star hotels.*

- There are some irregular adjectives

good	→	better	→	best
bad	→	worse	→	worst
far	→	further	→	furthest

▶ For more information turn to page 127.

practice   **11** Complete the text using comparatives, superlatives, *as ... as*, or *not as ... as*.

Getting Around Amsterdam

TRAMS
The tram is (*convenient*) the most covenient [1] form of transport. The Circle Line 20 is (*popular*) ....[2] line for tourists because it is (*easy*) ....[3] to move between attractions without changing lines.

BUSES
The buses generally start from Centraal Station and serve areas that are (*far*) ....[4] from the city centre.

TICKETS
Tickets can be bought on the trams and buses but (*cheap*) ....[5] way to travel is to buy a *strippenkaart*, a strip of fifteen tickets, sold at tourist offices and newsagent's.

BICYCLES
Amsterdam is a city for bicycles and more and more tourists are adopting this way of exploring the city. Remember always to ride on the right and that trams have priority if only because they are a lot (*big*) ....[6] you!

WALKING
(*good*) ....[7] way to see Amsterdam is on foot. Almost everything of interest is within comfortable walking distance. But a word of warning – walking is (*not safe*) ....[8] in other cities – watch out for the almost silent trams and stay out of the cycle lanes!

BY CANAL
And finally, what could be (*enjoyable*) ....[9] a trip on a canal boat? Boat trips are (*suitable*) ....[10] for people with limited time to explore the city and for the elderly and families with young children.

speaking   **12** Compare three hotels in your town. Include the following.

| size | price | location | facilities | special features | restaurant |

13 **Look at this information about hotels in Venice. Replace the words in italics with the adjectives in the box. Use a dictionary to help you.**

famous	high-class	historic	excellent	modern	attractive
spacious	value for money	charming	impeccable	delightful	

Venice's Best Hotels

H OTELS IN VENICE range from the luxurious and renowned, which are mainly clustered along the Grand Canal, to simple, family-run places in the quieter parts of the city.

1 Giorgione
This *quality*, *large* hotel, with its *good* facilities, offers every *new* comfort at lower prices than others of similar standard.

5 La Residenza
This family-run hotel offers *economy* and is away from the crowds. It has frescoed public rooms and antiques, but the bedrooms are more simple.

2 Flora
A flower-filled garden is just one of the attractions of this *nice* hotel.

3 Agli Alboretti
This *nice* hotel in a central location has *nice* rooms and a garden courtyard.

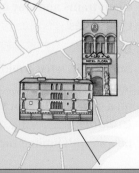

4 Gritti Palace
One of Venice's most *well-known* hotels, the Gritti offers rooms and service of *perfect* standard in an *old* palazzo on the Grand Canal.

Professional practice Dealing with new words

Try to guess the meaning of a word before you look it up in the dictionary or ask your teacher. We can guess the meaning of words from other words in a text.

* Is it an adjective, noun or verb?
* Does it have a positive or a negative meaning?
* Is it formal or informal?
* Is there a picture to help you guess?

Look at the hotel Agli Alboretti. What do you think *charming* means? What kind of a word is it? (Verb, adjective ...?) Find a similar word in the box opposite.

Do the same thing for other words you don't know in the hotel descriptions.

speaking **14** Work in pairs. Student A turn to page 115. Student B look at the information below and ask your partner for information about the hotel Giorgione. Then answer your partner's questions. Write five sentences comparing the hotels.

Europa e Regina

Calle Larga XXII Marzo, San Marco 2159.

📞 041 520 04 77 **FAX** 041 523 15 33

@ marcomilocco@sheraton.com

Rooms: 182 🛏 [1] 🛁 🔼 [TV] 🗒
🍴 🏊 boat service, private beach 🏷
€€€€€

The Europa offers the best value of all the deluxe hotels. The rooms are large and many of them have views across the Grand Canal. The magnificent public rooms are sumptuously ornate in typical Venetian style. There is a garden where people can eat and drink and a canalside terrace with breathtaking views.

writing **15** Find information about a hotel in Amsterdam or Venice on the internet. Write an email giving general information about the hotel in reply to an enquiry. Use positive adjectives and remember to include the following.

| rooms | facilities | location | price | restaurant | special features |

Consolidation ①

Present simple and continuous

1 **Lisa is working as a receptionist for the summer in a hotel in Stockholm. Complete her letter with the correct form of the verbs in brackets.**

Hello Maribel,

How are you? I (enjoy) __'m enjoying__ ¹ my new job – it's very interesting and varied and I (meet) _____² lots of people. The hotel is little but everyone here is well qualified and the standard of service is high. It's a good hotel – they (have) _____³ lots of facilities for children and disabled people. The staff (know) _____⁴ lots of languages so I (not / learn) _____⁵ very much Swedish because everyone (speak) _____⁶ to me in perfect English. Stockholm is a fantastic place. The city is on fourteen islands and the Stockholm archipelago has 24,000 islands! I (plan) _____⁷ to visit the main ones when I can but I (not / have) _____⁸ a lot of free time. What (you / do) _____⁹ this summer? (you / want) _____¹⁰ to visit me and we can explore the city and the islands together? Write soon –

Lisa

Past simple

2 **Complete the sentences with the correct form of the verbs in brackets.**

Rachel What (you / do) ___did you do___¹ last weekend, Sophie?

Sophie I (go) _____² to Amsterdam with Neil.

Rachel Really? How long (you / stay) _____³?

Sophie Oh, just for a long weekend. We (stay) _____⁴ in a hotel called the Prinsenhof.

Rachel (you / do) _____⁵ anything special?

Sophie Yes, we (meet) _____⁶ some old friends and we (see) _____⁷ a lot of art exhibitions. We (not / have) _____⁸ time to see Anne Frank's house. Oh, and we (have) _____⁹ a lot of Thai food.

Rachel (you / eat) _____¹⁰ Thai food in Holland!

Sophie That's right. There are a lot of Thai restaurants near the centre. (you / do) _____¹¹ anything special, Rachel?

Comparatives and superlatives

3 Complete the text with the correct comparative or superlative form of the words in brackets.

What to do and see in Miami

Downtown Miami is a combination of shiny high rises and busy discount stores. The fifty-five-storey First Union Financial Center, (*tall*) _the tallest_ [1] structure south of Atlanta, dominates the skyline. The water taxi will pick you up at one of ten points along the water in downtown Miami and South Beach. It's not (*practical*) ....[2] means of transport, but the views are great and it's (*exciting*) ....[3] than taking a bus. The Museum of Contemporary Art, inaugurated in 1996, is Miami's (*new*) ....[4] museum. MOCA exhibits (*late*) ....[5] contemporary art, including installations, multimedia shows and manipulated photography. Miami Beach is one of (*popular*) ....[6] resorts in the USA and South Beach is at its centre. Covering more than a square mile, it has (*big*) ....[7] concentration of art deco buildings in the world. Ocean Drive is its main promenade, with pastel-coloured hotels on one side and (*fantastic*) ....[8] beach on the other.

Countable and uncountable nouns

4 Are these words countable, uncountable or both? Put them in the correct groups.

| tourism | service | facility | information | accommodation | advice |
| furniture | towel | soap | sheet | luggage | bag |

countable	both	uncountable
facility	service	tourism

Now use the words to complete these sentences.

1 There isn't any ...._soap_........ in the bathroom but there are some ....

2 It is difficult to find .... in Amsterdam in the summer. All the hotels are full.

3 The hotel has a lot of .... for disabled guests.

4 The travel agent gave the customer some useful .... about where to go for her holiday.

5 The transport strike on Majorca last year had a serious effect on .... on the island.

6 I never take a lot of .... on holiday with me. I usually only pack one ....

5 Read the following letter of complaint. Why are the guests dissatisfied? What would they like in return?

Dear Sir / Madam,

We are writing to complain about our holiday in Venice. We stayed in the 'four-star' Hotel Rialto in June. The travel agent told us it would be fine at that time of year, but it was not 'sunny': it rained every day and the streets were flooded. As a result, we couldn't walk about the famous streets of Venice.

Your brochure said that 'rooms overlook a canal' but our room overlooked a narrow street with a view of a brick wall. Your brochure also said the hotel had beautiful antique Venetian furniture – our room only had an uncomfortable bed and an old chair. When we complained to the receptionist, she offered us a suite – at an additional charge!

In a four-star hotel I expect to find a satellite TV, but there wasn't one in our room. When we asked the receptionist, she said there weren't any TVs in the hotel and that we could watch TV at home. In addition to all these problems, room service was too slow.

In conclusion, our holiday to Venice was ruined by all these inconveniences. We are very unhappy with the service we received and we would like our money back. We await your reply and our compensation.

Yours faithfully,
Peter and Amy Harrison

6 Translate Mr and Mrs Harrison's letter of complaint into your own language. Use the tips below and a dictionary to help you.

Professional practice Translation

The following tips are useful when translating a text.
- read the whole text carefully before you start translating
- translate the general sense of each sentence, not every single word
- use good monolingual and bilingual dictionaries such as the *Longman WordWise Dictionary*
- read your finished translation — does it sound natural in your own language?
- check the final text for any errors

writing   **7 Use the information and tips below to reply to the Harrisons' letter.**

Special weekend rates! Venice – 3 nts in 4-star hotel.

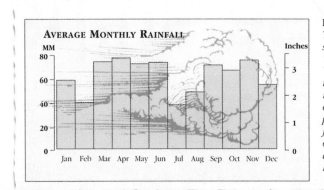

Rainfall Chart
The mountains and sea combine to give Venice and the Veneto higher rainfall than is normal in the rest of Italy, with the possibility of rain on just about any day of the year. The driest months are February and July.

Write to Mr and Mrs Harrison.
1   Send copy of the rainfall chart, explaining that it often rains in June.
2   The brochure says the suites overlook the canal, not the other rooms. (They were offered a suite, but said it was too expensive.) Antiques in reception area, not in rooms.
3   Brochure says the Rialto has a policy of no TVs – part of its charm.
4   Apologise but explain we are not able to return their money – the Rialto was a weekend offer at special rates.
The Manager

Professional practice Letters of apology

The following phrases are useful when responding to a written complaint.

- show sympathy
  We are very sorry to hear that you did not enjoy your

- apologise
  We apologise for any inconvenience caused, but

- give explanations
  We are writing to explain a few points
  Firstly, we are afraid that we are not responsible for
  Secondly,
  Finally,

- offer compensation if necessary
  Please accept our apologies and an offer of ...

- close with a formal salutation
  Yours sincerely

▶ For more information turn to page 110.

speaking   **8 Work in pairs. Practise dealing with complaints. Student A, you are a receptionist. Turn to page 117. Student B, you are a guest. Turn to page 119.**

Cruise ships

6

speaking **1** Work in pairs. What are the advantages and disadvantages of cruise holidays? Would your partner like to go on one? Where to?

reading **2** Complete the magazine article on the opposite page with these headings.

a) How do I get a job?

b) What kind of contracts are on offer?

c) What is a cruise holiday?

d) What is the pay like?

e) Who do the cruise lines employ?

3 Which of these people would be suitable to work on a cruise ship? Look at the text and give reasons for your answers.

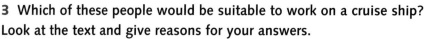

Teresa Merrick: I was fifty last month. I work as a nurse in an old people's home but it's very hard work at my age. I've always loved my holidays abroad. I'm studying French and Spanish at evening classes. I'll talk to anyone and I'm a capable and reliable worker.

Mario Vega: I like to finish work punctually so I can see my daughters before they go to bed. I'm not a very sociable person – I like to work in my garden at weekends and watch a film on TV in the evening. I'm a very responsible person.

Martin Lee: I'm twenty-two and studying at university. I help in my parents' restaurant at the weekends. In my free time I love playing football, going out with my friends and partying. I like meeting new people. I'd like a job for the summer.

Cruise monthly

The five most popular questions about cruise ship jobs

1 **What is a cruise holiday?**

Cruise ships are floating resorts – complete cities at sea. A typical cruise ship has a dozen decks and hundreds of cabins. A cruise vacation is about fun, entertainment, service and worldwide travel. There are more than 300 types of job aboard ship. Imagine yourself travelling to places you've always dreamed of and being paid for it.

2 ....?

Students, retired people, career changers, 'people people' who enjoy working with others. Cruise lines are always hiring people with experience in hospitality, tourism, entertainment, restaurants and bars, teaching, childcare, sales, customer relations, fitness, health and beauty, healthcare, finance and administration. Cruise lines hire dependable, competent people with outgoing, positive attitudes.

3 ....?

Familiarise yourself with the cruise companies. Where do their ships travel? What facilities do they have on board? And most importantly, what kind of passengers will you find on their ships? Choose several jobs that interest you and compare your qualifications and experience with the duties and responsibilities of the job. Learn what you need to add to your CV. For example, study a foreign language.

Sell yourself! Target your CV and covering letter to one specific job and show how your work experience, talents, skills and education relate to it. Show how you can contribute to the passengers' cruise experience.

4 ....?

The cruise industry hires year-round and seasonally. Most employees work for six to nine months with one or two months off. Many departments need extra crew in peak sailing periods.

5 ....?

Cruise ship pay compares well with similar jobs ashore plus you save a lot of money because most expenses are left behind. On board ship your room and meals are included.

Adapted from http://www.cruiseserver.net

vocabulary **Cruises**

4 Match the words from the text with their definitions.

1	deck	a)	money people spend while doing their work
2	cabin	b)	floor or platform built into a ship
3	entertainment	c)	on a boat
4	cruise lines	d)	room in a ship where passengers sleep
5	fitness	e)	people who work on a boat, ship or aeroplane
6	on board	f)	movement across water in a boat or ship
7	crew	g)	anything people watch for pleasure: shows, films
8	sailing	h)	on land
9	ashore	i)	companies that have a number of cruise ships
10	expenses	j)	physical exercise to keep you healthy

speaking **5 Would you like to work on a cruise ship? What job would you like to do?**

6 Look at the picture of the cruise ship *Oriana*. What kind of facilities do you think there are on board?

vocabulary Cabin facilities

7 Label the pictures with words from the box.

| twin bed 6 | porthole | balcony | Pullman berth | coffee table |
| sofa | curtains | ladder | drawers | armchair |

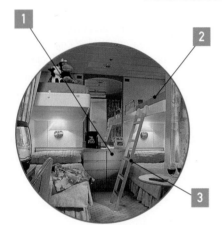

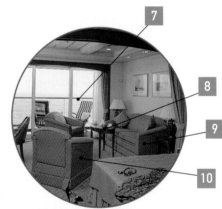

Inside twin with Pullman berths   Outside twin cabin   Mini-suite with balcony

speaking **8** Work in pairs. Student A turn to page 116. Student B turn to page 114. Look at the outside twin cabin and mini-suite on the cruise ship *Arcadia*. What are the differences between the two types of accommodation?

listening Announcements

9 Listen to the announcements and conversations aboard the *Oriana*. Match them with the parts of the ship shown below.

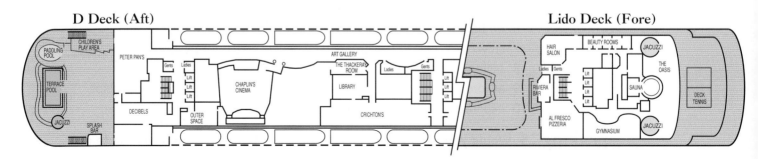

D Deck (Aft)   Lido Deck (Fore)

Language focus Present perfect

Look at the examples and match them with the uses below.

1 *The ballroom dancing competition **has started** on the Prom deck.*
2 *If you **haven't met** the captain yet, this is an ideal opportunity.*
3 *And **have** you ever **been** to the Greek islands?*

The present perfect can describe

a) a life experience
b) something that has never happened (often with *yet*)
c) a recent event

▶ For more information turn to page 127.

practice **10 Complete the conversation with the correct form of the verbs in brackets.**

Purser Have you welcomed the passengers, Sarah?
Sarah Yes, I have, sir.
Purser (*you / show*) Have you shown ¹ them to their cabins yet? And (*you / check*) ....² all their boarding passes?
Sarah Yes, sir.
Purser (*you / log*) ....³ all the passports into the computer?
Sarah Err, no, sir, I (*not*) ....⁴.
Purser And (*you / meet*) ....⁵ the captain?
Sarah No, sir, I (*not / meet*) ....⁶ the captain yet.
Purser Well, he's busy now. I'll introduce you to him later.
Sarah Very good, sir.
Purser That reminds me, Sarah, (*you / take*) ....⁷ your sea-sickness pills yet?
Sarah Yes, sir, I (*already / take*) ....⁸ them.
Purser Good. And (*Kelly / show*) ....⁹ you the emergency exits?
Sarah No, sir, she (*not*) ....¹⁰.

pronunciation **Contractions**

11 Listen to the contractions in these sentences. Mark them and then practise saying the sentences.

1 It is very near.
2 They are going to Antigua.
3 You are not going to Capri.
4 I have been to Santorini.
5 She has not been there yet.
6 We have already been there.
7 He is not going to the Seychelles.
8 We have been to Luxor and Karnak so far.

speaking **12 Work in pairs. Find an example of each of the following.**

a country you have both visited   a drink you have both had on holiday
a foreign dish you have both tried   a book you have both read

How to write a CV

13 Listen to a lecturer giving advice about writing CVs and complete the information below. Is the advice true for your country?

Professional practice Writing a CV (curriculum vitae)

ACE — the CV checklist

Appearance
- Is it no more than ...one... ...side... of A4 paper?
- Do you .... yourself by including all your .... experience?

Clarity
- Do your personal details appear .... of the page?
- Are your qualifications and jobs in .... chronological order?
- Are the .... and grammar correct?

Emphasis
- Does it show your .... both in and out of work?
- Does it give a good first impression of you?

The people who get .... are the ones who write the .... CVs!

---

14 Look at the CV below. How could Carla improve her CV?

Curriculum Vitae

Carla Hennessy

Education and Qualificationss
1998 – GNVQ Leisure and Tourism Diploma, Acton Tertiary College, London.
1996 – 4 GCSEs: english, french, maths and biology, Acton Comprehensive School.

Employment history
1996 to 1998 – shoe shop assistant (Saturdays only), Beta Shoes, Ealing, London.
1999 to present date – cocktail waitress, Magpie Hotel, Ealing, London.
1998 – aerobics instructor, Acton Vale Youth Club, London.

Additionl Information
I am a member of an amateur theatre group. I have quite good computing skills.

Personal Detials
Address: 131 Nelson Court, London W6, England.
Date of Birth: 13/3/1982
Telephone number: (0044) 020 7946 0006
Email: clhennessy@mhp.uk

---

15 Work in pairs. Interview your partner and find out enough information to write his / her CV. Then write the CV for your partner. For more information, turn to page 108.

16 When applying for a job you should always send a covering letter with your CV. Use the information below to write a covering letter for one of these jobs. For more information turn to page 109.

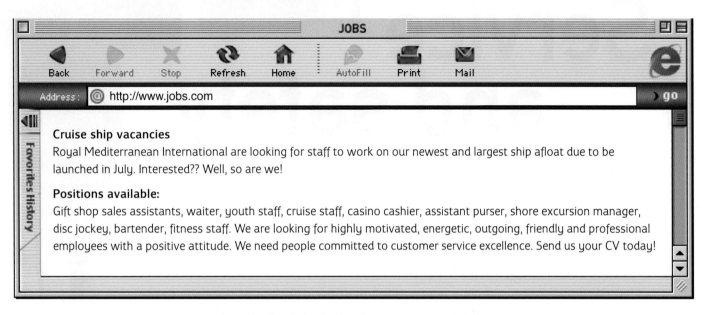

Cruise ship vacancies

Royal Mediterranean International are looking for staff to work on our newest and largest ship afloat due to be launched in July. Interested?? Well, so are we!

Positions available:

Gift shop sales assistants, waiter, youth staff, cruise staff, casino cashier, assistant purser, shore excursion manager, disc jockey, bartender, fitness staff. We are looking for highly motivated, energetic, outgoing, friendly and professional employees with a positive attitude. We need people committed to customer service excellence. Send us your CV today!

Professional practice Covering letters

The following phrases are useful when writing covering letters.

- say where you saw the advertisement
  I'm writing in reply to your advertisement in the (name of newspaper).

- say what job you are interested in
  I would like to apply for the position of (job title).

- emphasise what makes you the right person for the job
  I have experience in (types of duties and responsibilities).
  I am a (positive adjectives to describe you) *person.*

- say when you can attend an interview
  I am available for interview (days and times).

- write a concluding sentence
  I look forward to hearing from you.

speaking **17** Work in pairs. Student A, turn to page 116. Student B, you are the Human Resources Manager for Royal Mediterranean International and are going to interview someone who has replied to your advertisement.

- read the applicant's CV and covering letter and prepare questions.
  Why do you want this job?   Have you had any experience of cruise ships?
- greet the applicant and introduce yourself
  How do you do?   My name's ..., I'm the Human Resources Manager.
- ask the questions you have prepared
  I'd like to ask you a few questions. First of all ...

Service and safety

speaking

1 Work in pairs. What jobs do these pictures show? What services do these people provide for hotel guests?

listening

Checking in

2 Two guests check in at the reception of the Cape Grace Hotel in Cape Town, South Africa. Listen and put the following actions in the correct order. Is the receptionist polite?

- ☐ a) requests the guests' passports
- ☐ b) informs the guests of the check-out time
- ☐ c) asks the guests their names
- ☐1☐ d) greets the guests
- ☐ e) advises them about the time for breakfast
- ☐ f) checks how to spell their surname
- ☐ g) gives the room number and directions
- ☐ h) offers to have a porter carry their luggage

3 Look at the following advice for dealing with guests. What is considered polite in your country? How is it different from other cultures?

Professional practice Dealing with guests

When dealing with guests you should always:

- address a guest by his / her title and surname or say *sir* or *madam*
- show that you are listening and understand
- be patient and answer all the guest's questions
- say *please* when asking the guest for something
- say *thank you* when the guest replies

Language focus Modal verbs (requests and offers)

Look at the examples and complete the information below.

- Making polite requests
  Could you spell your surname for me, sir?
  Would you mind showing me your passports, please?
  Do you mind waiting here?

  Could you + ..._infinitive_.....?
  Would you mind + ...?
  Do you mind + ...?

- Making polite offers
  Would you like me to call your room?
  Would you like the porter to help with your luggage?

  Would you like + ... + ...+ ....?

▶ For more information turn to page 128.

practice

4 Complete the dialogue with polite questions.

Receptionist	_Can I help you, sir?_..............................[1]
Guest	Yes, I'd like to check in, please.
Receptionist	Certainly, sir. ....[2]
Guest	It's Van Rooyen.
Receptionist	Ah yes, Mr Van Rooyen. Single room for two nights. ....[3]
Guest	Non-smoking, please.
Receptionist	..............................[4]
Guest	Yes, here it is.
Receptionist	Thank you. I need to put your details into the computer.
Guest	That's OK. I don't need my passport right now so I can leave it with you and come and get it later this evening.
Receptionist	That'll be fine. ....[5]
Guest	Oh, yes please. They're a bit heavy. Thanks.

pronunciation

Sounding polite

5 Listen to the way the speaker's voice rises and falls in these sentences. Then practise saying the sentences politely.

1 Could you spell your surname for me, sir?
2 Would you mind showing me your passports, please?
3 Could you sign here please, madam?
4 Do you mind waiting a moment?
5 Would you like me to call your room?
6 Do you mind not smoking here?

6 Work in pairs. Student A, you are the receptionist at a hotel in your city. Student B, you are a guest at check-in. Role-play the check-in procedure.

Health and safety advice

7 Work in pairs. How safe is your town or city for tourists? What kind of crimes happen?

8 Mr and Mrs O'Donnell talk to the receptionist at the Cape Grace Hotel. Listen to their conversation and answer these questions.

1 What are Mr and Mrs O'Donnell going to do?
2 What does Beverley tell them not to take?
3 Where is Mr O'Donnell going to leave his camera?
4 What advice does Beverley give them about their car?
5 Where does Beverley tell them not to go?
6 What does Mrs O'Donnell want to visit?

9 Match the words with their definitions.

1 precautions	a) security device that needs a key
2 pickpocket	b) actions to stop something from happening
3 jewellery	c) strong metal container to keep valuable things in
4 safe-deposit box	d) valuable ornaments that people wear
5 lock	e) small, solid piece of medicine
6 pill	f) person who steals from people's bags and pockets

Language focus Giving safety advice

The following phrases are useful when giving advice.

You must take a few precautions.
I recommend you use traveller's cheques or credit cards.
You shouldn't take large amounts of cash.
You should try not to attract attention.
Avoid walk**ing** around the poorer areas of the city.
It's best to book with an organised tour.
It's a good idea to take a pill if you get seasick.

▶ For more information turn to page 128.

On safari

10 Match the words with their definitions.

1 ensure	a) routine, normal way of doing something
2 regulations	b) make certain that something happens
3 allow	c) long, thin creature with no legs
4 habit	d) keep something in its present condition
5 match	e) give permission
6 conserve	f) official rules
7 poison	g) something used to light cigarettes
8 snake	h) dangerous substance that can kill people

speaking   **11** Work in pairs. Student A, you want to visit the Kruger National Park. Student B, you are a hotel receptionist. Read the information below and give the guest advice.

Kruger is South Africa's largest national park and one of the best places to see wildlife in the world. To ensure that visitors are safe and conserve the park, some regulations are necessary. It is important not to drive fast because the animals also use the roads. Visitors are not allowed to leave their cars except at the special picnic areas. It is also possible to book guided safaris. Do not give food to the animals because it changes the animals' natural habits and can produce aggression.

Wildlife gathers at the waterhole in Kruger National Park

Forest and bush fires are a major danger, especially during the dry winter months. So don't throw away burning matches or cigarette ends. Always protect yourself from the sun with a hat and sunblock. Most snakes in South Africa are not poisonous but watch where you put your hands and feet when on safari. Malaria is still common in the Mpumalanga region where the park is located so take precautions.

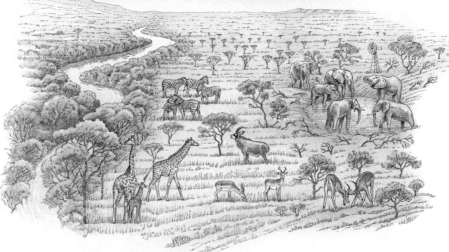

Rangers have to limit the number of elephants, impala and giraffes that the park can support by moving young animals to other reserves.

webtask   **Health and safety advice**

12 What health and safety advice is there on the internet about your city or country? Do you agree with the advice? Write your own advice for visitors.

Guest questionnaire

13 Read the guest satisfaction questionnaire from the Safari Experience Hotel. Match these quotes with what the guest wrote in the questionnaire (1–6).

a) There was a dirty black ring around the bath and I had wet towels for a week.

b) I couldn't sleep at night because it was so hot.

c) We waited an hour for the bus to arrive because we were told the wrong time.

d) They never said *good morning* or smiled. One porter told me he was too busy to take my luggage.

e) The guide wouldn't go anywhere near the animals. He didn't even know what some of them were called!

f) I had to wait forty-five minutes for a sandwich. When it came, it wasn't the one I ordered.

> Paula, urgent! Write a
> letter of apology to the
> guest immediately.
> Offer one night for
> free. Leave a copy on
> my desk.
> Thanks.

SAFARI EXPERIENCE HOTEL

We would be grateful if you could spend just a few minutes of your time completing this questionnaire. We aim to provide you with the best accommodation and service possible. Many thanks for staying at the Safari Experience Hotel.

Reception	Poor	Average	Good
Reception desk	✔		
Concierge		✔	
Porter	✔		

1 Staff were generally unfriendly and sometimes rude.

2 The receptionist did not give us the correct times for the different excursions available.

Rooms	Poor	Average	Good
Comfort	✔		
Chambermaids	✔		
Maintenance	✔		

3 The chambermaids were inefficient.

4 When the air conditioning broke down, they said it couldn't be repaired until the following day

Room service	Poor	Average	Good
Quality		✔	
Waiting staff	✔		
Laundry		✔	

5 The waiter did not bring the correct order and the service was extremely slow.

Excursions	Poor	Average	Good
Quality	✔		
Variety	✔		
Guides	✔		

6 The guide seemed inexperienced and did not know the names of the animals.

Please leave this questionnaire at reception when you check out. Thank you.

listening **Giving reasons**

14 Listen to the staff of the Safari Experience speak to Paula, the Manager, about the problems. Match the explanations to the action that Paula needs to take. Who did she speak to?

a) need for training in customer relations

b) update brochure

c) improve restaurant service – employ more staff

d) employ more experienced safari guides

writing **Letter of apology**

15 Complete Paula's letter of apology to the guest using the following expressions.

please find enclosed	we were very sorry to hear
we need to improve	we apologise for any inconvenience
we would like to offer you	unfortunately

When replying to a complaint always:

- show sympathy
- apologise
- give an explanation
- promise action
- offer compensation

SAFARI EXPERIENCE HOTEL

Mr Roy Petersen
1422 Ocean Drive
Jacksonville
Florida
USA

10 October 2003

Dear Mr Petersen,

.....We were very sorry to hear.....[1] that you were unhappy with the Safari Experience Hotel. We always try to make all our guests feel welcome and to provide a quality service at all times.

We have spoken to the staff involved and it seems that we were fully booked at the time you stayed. ....[2], our usual safari guide was unwell, but has now returned to work. In addition, a number of our staff were not on duty because of the local holiday. We also take note of the fact that ....[3] our facilities.

....[4] our new brochure with the correct prices and times for safari excursions.

....[5] a double room for one night at no charge in compensation. Once again, ...,....................................[6] and hope you will stay at the Safari Experience Hotel in the future.

Yours sincerely,

P. Morgan.

Paula Morgan
Manager
Safari Experience Hotel

East meets West

speaking

1 Look at the pictures of Turkey on these two pages. What kind of tourist attractions do they show? What makes Turkey a popular holiday destination?

listening

A radio programme

2 Listen to the first part of a radio programme about holidays and complete the table.

	listener 1	listener 2	listener 3
destination	Corfu	....	....
reason	....	....	....

3 Now listen to the next part of the programme. Are these statements true or false? Correct any false statements.

1 Turkish beaches will be very crowded this year.
2 Lisa thinks Bodrum is the most interesting place in Turkey.
3 The name *Pamukkale* means 'Snow Castle' in Turkish.
4 You can't swim in the natural pools of Pamukkale.
5 Lisa thinks Turkey will be one of the top ten tourist destinations this year.
6 *Holiday Options* has a leaflet for listeners who want information about Turkey.

pronunciation **Connected speech**

4 **We often connect words by not pronouncing all the letters. Listen to these sentences and mark the connected words and any letters which are not pronounced.**

1 Good morning and welcome to *Holiday Options*.
2 Oh, it has got to be Majorca. I love it.
3 I've been to Majorca twice now.
4 Do you think Turkey will be popular this year?
5 And do you think Turkey might be a hot spot?

speaking **5** **Work in pairs. Which is the best tourist resort in your country? Consider the following and choose the most popular three resorts in your class.**

type of tourism	accommodation and facilities
value for money	transport location

My favourite resort in Turkey is Kas. It's the best resort because you can go on cruises and also visit the Greek ruins.
I think Bodrum is better than Kas because there are more hotels.

▼ Roman theatre at Ephesus

▲ Mineral pools at Pamukkale

Castle of St Peter ▶

Language focus Predictions and intentions

We can express future predictions and intentions in the following ways.

going to + infinitive

* We use *going to* for strong predictions based on present evidence.
  *Research says more people are **going to book** special activity holidays in future.*

* We also use *going to* for future plans.
  *I'm **going to fly** to Dalyan. (I've already bought the ticket.)*

* When we use *going to + go*, we often drop the infinitive.
  *A lot of people are **going to (go to)** Spain, Tenerife and the Balearic Islands.*

will / won't + infinitive

* We use *will / won't* for predictions, with or without present evidence.
  *Lisa thinks more tourists **will visit** Turkey this year.*
  *She thinks it probably **won't be** as popular as Spain or Greece.*

* We also use *will / won't* for decisions made at the time of speaking.
  *I don't have a favourite resort, but I'll probably **go** to the Mediterranean again.*

may / might + infinitive

* We use *may* or *might* when we are not sure what will happen.
  *Lisa thinks Turkey **might be** one of the top ten holiday destinations.*

▶ For more information turn to page 128.

practice   **6 Write predictions about Turkey. Sometimes more than one answer is possible.**

1 The metro system in Istanbul *is going to be* (be) extended.

2 I think the metro .... (*replace*) all the old trams in Istanbul.

3 More new restaurants and hotels .... (*be*) built to accommodate the increasing numbers of visitors.

4 They announced that the International Sailing Races .... (*be*) held again at Prince's Island in July.

5 Although Ankara is the capital of Turkey, it .... (*not / be*) as popular with tourists as Istanbul next year.

6 Have you seen the weather forecast? They say this summer .... (*be*) really hot with temperatures of up to forty-five degrees Centigrade.

7 Many locals .... (*not / stay*) in the city in the summer – they .... (*probably / go*) to the Black Sea beaches.

8 Istanbul .... (*probably / keep*) its mix of Asian and European cultures.

◀ The New Mosque

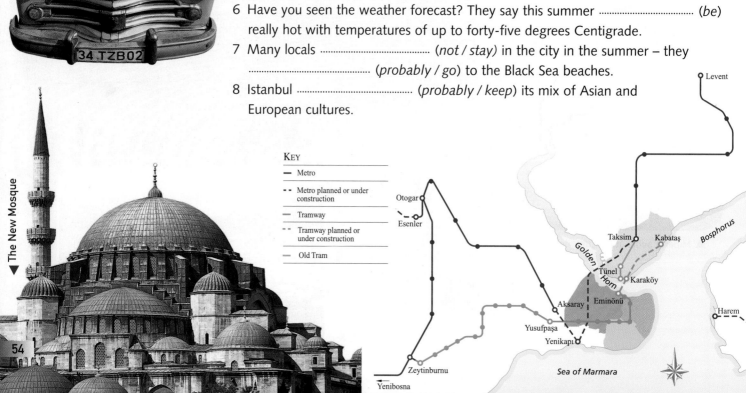

KEY

— Metro

-- Metro planned or under construction

— Tramway

-- Tramway planned or under construction

— Old Tram

speaking **Shopping in Istanbul**

7 Work in pairs. Look at the pictures. What kind of gifts or souvenirs would you buy in Istanbul's markets for the following people?

younger brother / sister	aunt and uncle	a classmate
mother and father	an elderly relative	your teacher

What to Buy in Istanbul

WITH ITS ENDLESS BAZAARS, markets, shops and stalls, Istanbul is a souvenir hunter's paradise. If you are seeking a bargain, jewellery and leather can be worth investing in.

Turkish delight
Delicious sweets such as halva, Turkish delight and baklava are very popular.

Blue and white plate
Ceramics form a major part of Turkey's artistic tradition. The style varies according to the area of origin.

Grand Bazaar
The largest market in the world, the Grand Bazaar contains about 4,000 shops.

Blue glass-eye pendants
Jewellery includes pendants made from gold, silver and other materials. A simple blue glass eye is said to protect you from evil.

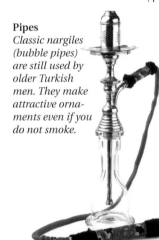

Pipes
Classic nargiles (bubble pipes) are still used by older Turkish men. They make attractive ornaments even if you do not smoke.

Handicrafts
Jewellery boxes crafted from wood or bone make unusual souvenirs.

Carpets
Most of the carpets offered for sale will be almost new. Antique carpets are far more expensive.

DK

webtask **Traditional gifts**

8 Find information about traditional gifts from three countries of your choice.

speaking **9** Work in pairs. What are your partner's plans for his / her next holiday?

where and when	length of stay	transport
the weather	holiday activities	accommodation	food

The future of tourism

10 Listen to four experts in the travel industry make predictions for the future of tourism. Match each speaker to one of the following subjects.

a) a new type of tourist

b) changes in the type of holidays

c) technological changes

d) changes in developing nations

11 Listen to the four speakers again. Are these statements true or false? Correct any false statements.

1 There will need to be more holidays for older tourists in future.

2 People will take longer holidays in future.

3 The cost of travel is predicted to increase.

4 The market for tourism will only increase in western countries.

5 The majority of people will not want mass-market holidays.

Change words

12 Match the words with opposite meanings.

1	go down	a)	long-term
2	further	b)	increase
3	more	c)	worse
4	growth	d)	nearer
5	short-term	e)	less / fewer
6	better	f)	reduction

The Hermosa development

13 Hermosa is a beautiful island whose government wants to increase tourism. Look at the map on the opposite page. Listen to a development proposal and mark the sites on the map. Then answer the questions.

1 How will visitors get to the island?

2 Where is the new resort going to be built?

3 What will the new visitors' centre have?

4 What types of accommodation will there be?

5 What is the main benefit of the proposal?

Professional practice Giving presentations (1)

Look at the tapescript on pages 137—138 and complete these phrases.

- introduce yourself and what you are going to talk about

  I'm Carlos Alvarez and I'm a member of .... the Hermosa Tourist Board.

  .... *our proposal for a new resort on the island.*

  .... *how tourists will get to the island.*

  .... *the location of the new resort.*

  .... *accommodation.*

- present the advantages and disadvantages of each point

  .... *the monuments are the most famous sight.*

- give your conclusion

  .... *we think that the resort by the monuments is the best option.*

speaking **14** Work in groups. You are the Hermosa Tourist Board. Look at the map and choose one of the possible sites for development. Then prepare and give a presentation to support your choice. Consider the following points.

Proposal 1
The quiet fishing port on the east coast where most of the islanders live.

Proposal 2
Beaches to the north – no roads to the area and no buildings or facilities there at the moment.

Proposal 3
Delta in the south of the island close to the fishing port and where many unusual species of birds can be seen.

Transport
How will holidaymakers get to and around the island?
- airport
- ferry service
- new roads for cars and buses
- car rental, bicycle and motorbike hire services

Entertainment / activities
- historical / sightseeing trips
- bars and restaurants
- water sports
- hiking

Accommodation
- hotels and hostels
- camp sites
- self-catering apartments
- rooms in family homes

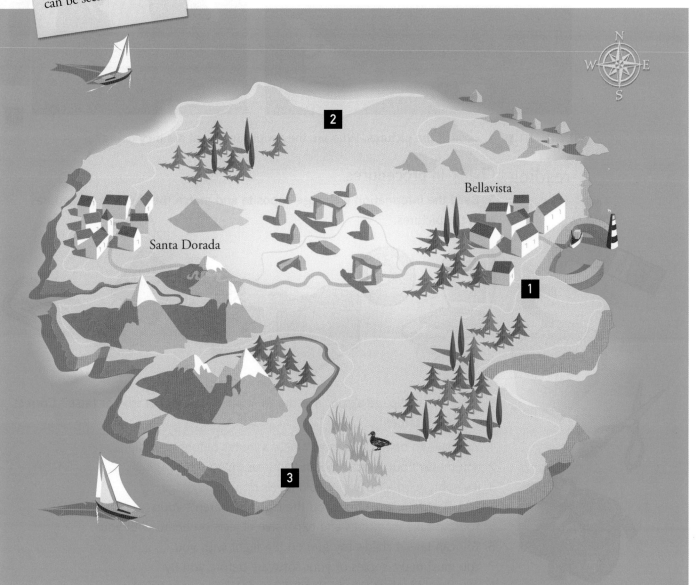

9

Window seat or aisle?

speaking **1** Look at the pictures. Who are the people and what are they doing?

reading **Check-in procedures**

2 Read the information webpage opposite and match the check-in procedures with the pictures.

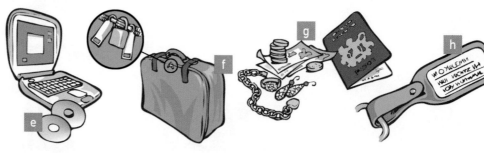

3 Read the webpage again. Are the following statements true or false? Correct any false statements.

1 You have to be at the airport ninety minutes before your flight.
2 You mustn't put your name and address on your luggage.
3 It's not a good idea to have old labels on your luggage.
4 You can't take any objects on the flight that aren't yours.
5 You can take medicines and expensive objects on board with you.
6 You can take a child's toy gun on the flight with you.
7 You must make copies of your software before you fly.
8 You should look at the destination tag details on your ticket.

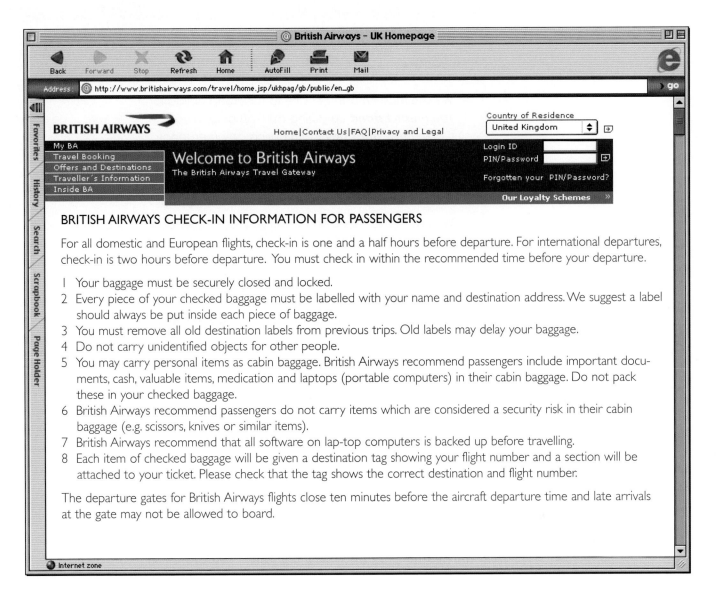

BRITISH AIRWAYS CHECK-IN INFORMATION FOR PASSENGERS

For all domestic and European flights, check-in is one and a half hours before departure. For international departures, check-in is two hours before departure. You must check in within the recommended time before your departure.

1 Your baggage must be securely closed and locked.
2 Every piece of your checked baggage must be labelled with your name and destination address. We suggest a label should always be put inside each piece of baggage.
3 You must remove all old destination labels from previous trips. Old labels may delay your baggage.
4 Do not carry unidentified objects for other people.
5 You may carry personal items as cabin baggage. British Airways recommend passengers include important documents, cash, valuable items, medication and laptops (portable computers) in their cabin baggage. Do not pack these in your checked baggage.
6 British Airways recommend passengers do not carry items which are considered a security risk in their cabin baggage (e.g. scissors, knives or similar items).
7 British Airways recommend that all software on lap-top computers is backed up before travelling.
8 Each item of checked baggage will be given a destination tag showing your flight number and a section will be attached to your ticket. Please check that the tag shows the correct destination and flight number.

The departure gates for British Airways flights close ten minutes before the aircraft departure time and late arrivals at the gate may not be allowed to board.

vocabulary **Check-in**

4 Match the words and definitions. Use a dictionary to help you.

1 departure lounge
2 delay
3 cabin
4 valuables
5 checked baggage
6 attached
7 gate
8 board

a) bags that do not go in the passenger cabin
b) area where passengers wait
c) connected
d) slow down or cause to be late
e) security area where you get on the plane
f) things that you own that cost a lot of money
g) get on a plane, train or boat
h) area in the plane where the passengers sit

speaking **5 Work in pairs. Student A you are the check-in attendant. Turn to page 117. Student B you are a passenger. Prepare a short dialogue going through the security procedures in the leaflet. Then present your dialogue to the class.**

Language focus Modal verbs (obligation)

don't have to	should / shouldn't	have to / must / mustn't

0 ├───┤ 100%

- We use *must / mustn't / have to* for strong obligation.
  You **mustn't stand up** during take-off or landing.
  Cabin crew **must stay** calm during an emergency.
  You **have to check in** two hours before the departure time.

- We also use *can't* for strong obligation.
  You **can't carry** dangerous articles in your luggage.

- We use *should / shouldn't* for strong recommendations or advice.
  Cabin crew **should be** friendly and good team workers.
  You **shouldn't drink** too much tea or coffee on the flight.

- We use *don't have to* for something that is not necessary.
  You **don't have to check in** two hours before departure on domestic flights.
  A flight attendant **doesn't have to know** how to fly the plane.

▶ For more information turn to page 129.

practice **6 Match the safety symbols with the regulations.**

1 You must fasten your seatbelt.
2 You can't smoke on this flight.
3 You can't use your mobile phone.
4 You mustn't inflate your life jacket while in the aircraft.
5 In case of emergencies, you should take off high-heeled shoes.
6 You should put any excess hand luggage under the seat in front of you.
7 You have to put hand luggage in the overhead locker.
8 You mustn't block the emergency exits.

speaking

7 **Work in pairs. Student B, turn to page 118. Student A, you are a flight attendant flying to London from New York. Use this information to answer a passenger's questions about various procedures on board the aircraft.**

- non-smoking flight
- no seats available in business class for economy class passengers
- vegetarian meals must be booked in advance
- if overhead locker for hand luggage full, put under seat
- no mobile phones
- laptops no problem
- landing card necessary for non-EU citizens

Flight information

8 **Look at the flight information screen and answer the questions.**

1 What is the abbreviation for Newark airport?
2 What is the abbreviation for London Heathrow?
3 What is the abbreviation for 'operated by'?
4 How many different airlines have flights to London?
5 What does the asterisk (*) mean?

```
Departing from New York on Sunday October 7


Depart  Arrive  From  To    Flight    OP BY  Gate    Remarks
18.35   06.35*  EWR   LHR   BA184  1   BA     45      BOARDING
18.55   06.55*  EWR   LHR   AA 092     AA          2          3
19.45   07.30*  EWR   LHR          4   UA     62          5
20.45   08.45*  EWR   LHR   BA 188     BA          6          7


* arrives one day later
```

listening   **Now listen to the airport announcements and complete the information.**

writing

9 **Work in groups. What advice or information would you give to a visitor to your country? Make a short information leaflet for tourists.**

- make a list of dos and don'ts
- put them into groups and a logical order
- think about the design of the leaflet
- draw your leaflet
- discuss where you would make the leaflet available

listening   Cabin crew training

10 Listen to David Torra, a BA flight attendant, talking about his five-week training course. When does each part of the training course happen?

	Week				
	1	2	3	4	5
How to read an airline ticket	✓	✓			
Different types of aircraft					
Collect new uniform					
Safety and emergency procedures					
Emergency flight simulations					
Medical training					
How to serve food and drink					
First real flight					

11 Listen again and answer the questions.

1 What safety equipment does David talk about?
2 What is a 'mockab'?
3 Who act as passengers?
4 What type of emergencies do they practise in the 'mockabs'?
5 How do the trainers simulate an emergency in the 'mockabs'?
6 What examples of medical emergencies does David talk about?
7 What do trainees do in the 'mockab' in the final week?
8 How long is the probation period?

listening **Selling duty-free**

12 Listen to David sell in-flight duty-free to a passenger and answer the questions.

1 What size is the perfume bottle?
2 How much is it in dollars?
3 What types of cuddly toy are there?
4 Which toy does the passenger buy?
5 How much did the passenger spend in total?

▲ Wilbur Bear

speaking **13 Work in pairs. Student A, you are a flight attendant. Turn to page 118. Student B, you are a passenger on a flight from the USA. Look at the duty-free brochure and buy something. Ask to pay in dollars.**

£20.00 / $30.00
Lancôme Eye Shadow Coffret
Mini colour focus eye shadows in an attractive coffret.

£59.00 / $88.00
Diesel Sunglasses
Metal rectangular sunglasses in matte black colour with lenses offering 100% UV protection.

£48.00 / $72.00
Swatch Skin Watch
Stainless steel linked bracelet waterproof to 30m.

£10.00 / $15.00
Westclox Trekmate Alarm Clock
Travel alarm with day/date function. Available in silver or graphite.

£20.00 / $30.00
Travel Wallet by Taurus
Taurus leather travel wallet. Features a flight ticket slip pocket, inside zip compartment and credit card section.

£20.00 / $30.00
Braun Oral-B Travel Toothbrush
Cleans better than a manual toothrush. Nine days continuous brushing from one full charge.

£10.00 / $15.00
British Airways Model Aircraft
Models require no glue or paint and simply snap together. Please ask your cabin crew to see the range.

10 Business or pleasure?

speaking

1 Work in pairs. Look at the pictures. What reasons for travel do they show? What other reasons for travel can you think of?

2 What are the needs of these types of travellers? Think of the following.

> transport   accommodation   catering   entertainment

3 Work in pairs. Discuss these questions.

1 Who travels more frequently, a holidaymaker or a businessperson?
2 Is a business traveller more likely to use a scheduled or charter flight?
3 What kind of hotel is a business traveller likely to stay in?
4 What forms of transport will a business traveller use?
5 Why are business travellers so important to travel agents, airlines and hotels?

vocabulary

Hotel facilities

4 Work in pairs. Decide which hotel facilities these symbols represent.

1	2	3	4	5	6	7	8	9	10
FAX			TV	24					

Which facilities are important to hotel guests if they are on a business trip?
What other facilities are important to these people when choosing a hotel?

reading   **5 Complete the webpage for the Forum Hotel in Cracow with the following titles.**

Meeting facilities   Accommodation   Facilities   Location   Dining   Leisure

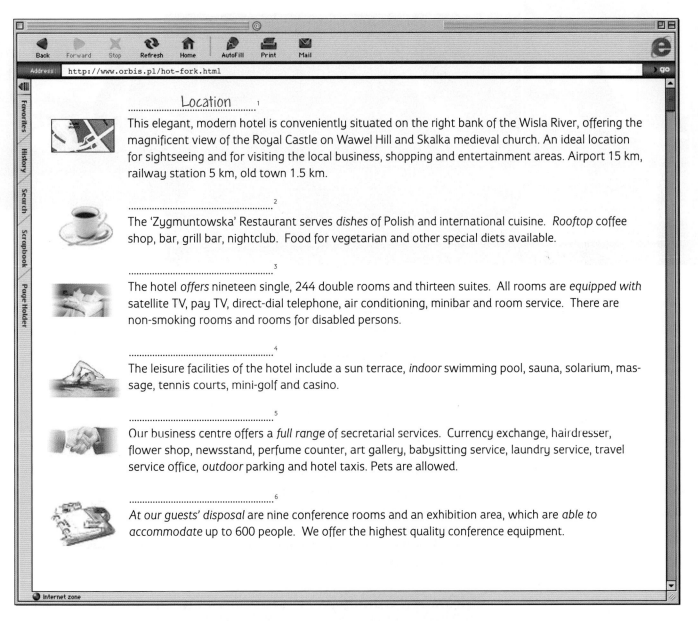

Address: http://www.orbis.pl/hot-fork.html

.... Location   1

This elegant, modern hotel is conveniently situated on the right bank of the Wisla River, offering the magnificent view of the Royal Castle on Wawel Hill and Skalka medieval church. An ideal location for sightseeing and for visiting the local business, shopping and entertainment areas. Airport 15 km, railway station 5 km, old town 1.5 km.

....   2

The 'Zygmuntowska' Restaurant serves *dishes* of Polish and international cuisine. *Rooftop* coffee shop, bar, grill bar, nightclub. Food for vegetarian and other special diets available.

....   3

The hotel *offers* nineteen single, 244 double rooms and thirteen suites. All rooms are *equipped with* satellite TV, pay TV, direct-dial telephone, air conditioning, minibar and room service. There are non-smoking rooms and rooms for disabled persons.

....   4

The leisure facilities of the hotel include a sun terrace, *indoor* swimming pool, sauna, solarium, massage, tennis courts, mini-golf and casino.

....   5

Our business centre offers a *full range* of secretarial services. Currency exchange, hairdresser, flower shop, newsstand, perfume counter, art gallery, babysitting service, laundry service, travel service office, *outdoor* parking and hotel taxis. Pets are allowed.

....   6

At our guests' disposal are nine conference rooms and an exhibition area, which are *able to accommodate* up to 600 people. We offer the highest quality conference equipment.

vocabulary   **6 Complete these sentences using the *italicised* words from the webpage.**

1 Some rooms are .....equipped with.... modem sockets and fax machines.

2 The .... restaurant has a fantastic view of the city.

3 The hotel .... a professional interpretation and translation service.

4 There is a .... of conference equipment.

5 The small conference room is .... a maximum of 100 delegates.

6 Vegetarian .... are also available.

7 There are both .... and .... exhibition areas.

8 There is a business centre .... from 9 am to 5 pm.

speaking   ## Recommending places to visit

7 Work in pairs. Look at the pictures of Cracow. Find out which three places your partner would like to visit and why.

listening   ## Where to go in Cracow

8 Listen to a hotel receptionist recommend places to visit in Cracow. Which of the places above does he recommend?

9 Listen again and answer the questions.

1 Why hasn't Laura got much time for sightseeing?
2 How long will it take to see the sights at the Wawel castle?
3 Why does the receptionist recommend going early to the castle?
4 What type of place is Pod Baranami?
5 Why doesn't Laura want to go there?
6 What does Laura decide to do in the evening?

10 Look at the tapescript on page 139 and underline all the phrases for making suggestions and recommendations.

Language focus   Modal verbs (*can*, *could* and *might*)

- We use *can* for possible options or simple facts.
  *If you want to visit Poland, you **can fly** to Warsaw or Cracow.*

- We use *can / could* for suggestions.
  *You **can / could have** lunch in a café in the main square.*

- We can also use *might* for recommendations.
  *You **might want** to go walking in the Carpathian mountains.*

- We use an infinitive after modal verbs but without *to*.
  *You **can / could ~~to~~ hire** a car and travel around the lakes.*

▶ For more information turn to page 129.

listening Wawel Hill

11 A tourist follows a tour of Wawel Hill. Listen and match the events with the dates and periods you hear. Where in the picture is the group standing?

1 Vistulan people inhabited Wawel Hill   a) in the 20th century.
2 The castle and cathedral were built   b) in the 17th and 18th centuries.
3 Warsaw became the capital of Poland   c) in ancient times.
4 Wawel Castle suffered political conflicts   d) at the beginning of the 17th century .
5 Wawel Castle was restored   e) in the late medieval period.

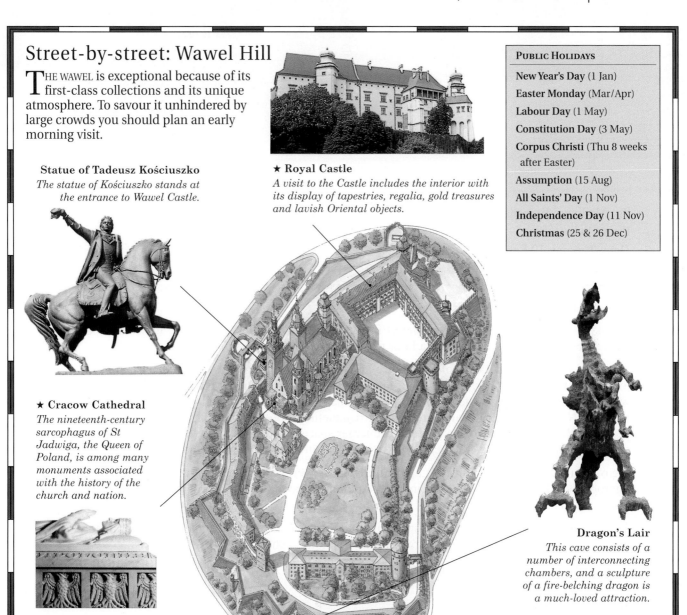

Street-by-street: Wawel Hill

THE WAWEL is exceptional because of its first-class collections and its unique atmosphere. To savour it unhindered by large crowds you should plan an early morning visit.

Statue of Tadeusz Kościuszko
The statue of Kościuszko stands at the entrance to Wawel Castle.

★ Cracow Cathedral
The nineteenth-century sarcophagus of St Jadwiga, the Queen of Poland, is among many monuments associated with the history of the church and nation.

★ Royal Castle
A visit to the Castle includes the interior with its display of tapestries, regalia, gold treasures and lavish Oriental objects.

PUBLIC HOLIDAYS
New Year's Day (1 Jan)
Easter Monday (Mar/Apr)
Labour Day (1 May)
Constitution Day (3 May)
Corpus Christi (Thu 8 weeks after Easter)
Assumption (15 Aug)
All Saints' Day (1 Nov)
Independence Day (11 Nov)
Christmas (25 & 26 Dec)

Dragon's Lair
This cave consists of a number of interconnecting chambers, and a sculpture of a fire-belching dragon is a much-loved attraction.

DK

speaking Cracow by night

12 Work in pairs. Student A, you are a hotel receptionist in Cracow. Turn to page 118. Student B, you are a guest at the hotel. Turn to page 123.

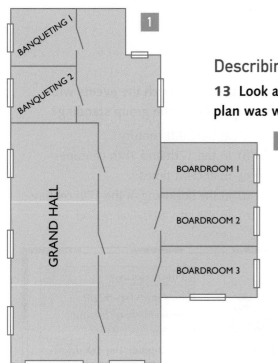

Describing conference facilities and services

13 Look at the fax describing the conference rooms at a hotel. Which floor plan was with the fax?

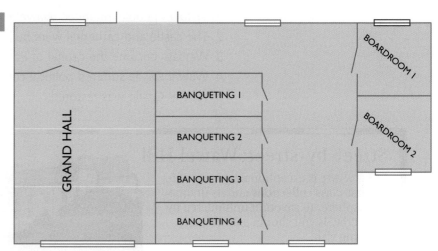

To: Ms Laura French   Fax: 0034 208 491 445
From: Sales Office
Date: Tuesday 12 September
Subject: Conference facilities   Pages: 2

Dear Ms French

Thank you for your email and your interest in our hotel. It is my pleasure to send information on our conference facilities along with a floor plan.

The hotel has a total of $700m^2$ of conference and banqueting space. The Conference Centre is located on the ground floor. It consists of nine meeting rooms, including the Grand Hall ballroom, which is able to accommodate up to 600 people. The room can be divided into three separate sections. Next to the Grand Hall there are four banqueting rooms, with capacity for about fifty people each. They can be connected to create larger spaces. There are also two boardrooms for smaller groups. The whole conference centre is air conditioned. Five rooms have daylight.

We offer a full range of technical equipment including overhead projector, slide projector, microphones, flip charts, lectern, audiovisual equipment, satellite link, internet access and computer rental.

The support services at our guests' disposal include: secretarial services, conference coordinator, interpreters, printing service, florist, transportation, photographers and catering services.

If you have any other questions, please let me know.

With kind regards,

Katarzyna Zarek
(Conference Bookings Manager)

vocabulary Conference equipment

14 Match the technical equipment with the pictures. Which support services do you think are essential? Which are optional extras?

> overhead projector   microphone   lectern   satellite dish
> flip chart   video conferencing equipment
> slide projector   computer

Professional practice Faxes and emails

Look at the fax on the opposite page and complete these phrases.

- opening a fax / email
  Dear .....Sir..... */ Madam,*
  Dear Ms / Mr / Mrs / ....,

- beginning the body of a fax
  Thank you for your .... *and your* .... *hotel.*
  It is my .... *to send you information* .... *our* .... *facilities.*

- ending the body of a fax
  If you .... *any other* ...., *please* ....
  Please do not hesitate to contact us if you have any questions.
  We look forward to hearing from you.

- closing a fax
  Yours sincerely / faithfully,
  With .... *regards,*

writing **15 Work in pairs or small groups. You receive a fax asking about your hotel's conference facilities. Write a reply and include the following information. Use the fax on page 111 to help you.**

- floor plan for the conference rooms
- number, size and capacity of conference rooms
- support services and equipment available

Consolidation ②

Giving advice

1 Complete the advice about youth hostelling with the phrases in the box.

> best to   shouldn't   best not to   recommend   a good idea to   avoid

1 It's <u>a good idea to</u> book youth hostels in advance, especially those in main cities.

2 It's .... get hostel membership before your trip.

3 It's .... carry a lot of cash on you.

4 We .... you take traveller's cheques with you and keep them in a money belt.

5 .... taking a sleeping bag. You have to use a sleep-sheet.

6 You .... take a lot of clothes with you because you won't be able to carry your backpack!

Past simple and present perfect

2 Complete the text about Yukio's inter-railing holiday with the past simple or present perfect form of the verbs in brackets.

Yukio and his friends are travelling around Central Europe by train. So far they (visit) <u>'ve visited</u> ¹ Poland where they (do) ....² some sightseeing in Cracow and (stay) ....³ in the mountains in Zakopane. They (not / visit) ....⁴ the Czech Republic yet. They're going to stay in Prague for a few days. There probably (not / be) ....⁵ any time to see Budapest but Yukio would like to go there in the future. Yukio and his friends are stopping in Germany and France on the way back home. Yukio's friends (never / be) ....⁶ to Berlin before. Yukio (go) ....⁷ to Berlin in the spring because his girlfriend is studying there with the Erasmus exchange programme.

Yukio (be / already) ....⁸ to France a few times. He (drive) ....⁹ from Spain to Paris last summer. Paris is very expensive but he always stays with his brother who lives there. His brother, Kazuo, (work) ....¹⁰ in a hotel in Paris since he finished university. Yukio (live) ....¹¹ in Tokyo all his life but he would like to work abroad when he's older.

speaking

3 Work in pairs. Find out the following information from your partner.

- How many foreign countries you / go to?
- When / you / go to ...?
- How long / you / stay there?
- What / you / do there?

A European tour

4 Work in pairs. Label these countries on the map of Europe. What tourist attractions do you know of in these countries?

Italy Poland Spain the Netherlands Germany

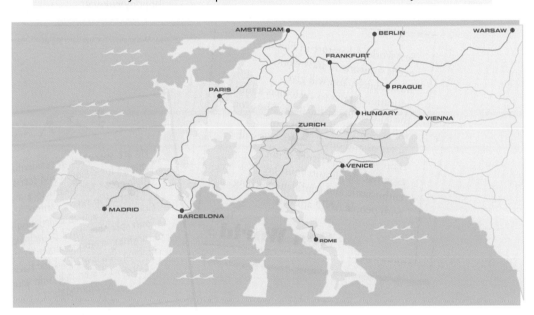

5 Plan a two-week rail trip around the five countries, starting on Saturday 17 May. Think about the following details and complete the itinerary below.

- where will your train journey start?
- which countries will you visit?
- how long will you stay in each country?
- which places would you most like to visit?
- where will your train journey end?

Destination:					
Arrive:					
Depart:					
Sights:					

speaking

6 Now talk to other students in the class about their plans. Who are you going to meet on your holiday and where?

Job applications

7 Match the jobs with the advertisements.

karaoke singer | hospitality staff water sports instructor
trainee croupier tour guide and shark feeder

1

Have you got the voice of an angel? A popular pub in Cyprus is looking for female singers to entertain holidaymakers.

2

Sea World Adventure in Florida needs someone to start work immediately. You will give educational talks to customers about the aquatic life at the park. Also, you will assist with the feeding of piranhas and other sea life. We will train you so experience is not essential. Applicants must be enthusiastic and confident working with people AND animals!

Sea World

3

We are specialists in residential activity courses for children and teenagers. We employ over 200 instructors a year and operate in twelve centres across Europe. As well as instructing in your own speciality, you'll be helping with anything from mountain biking to climbing. You'll get paid for having fun and we'll even help with your accommodation.

4

This is a great opportunity to get involved in the fast and exciting world of working in London casinos. This is where you'll learn to be the master of the roulette wheel. Applicants must be numerate, with good customer service skills and smart appearance.

QUEEN *Casinos*

5

WE ARE LOOKING FOR EIGHTEEN TO THIRTY YEAR OLDS TO JOIN OUR TEAM. STAFF MAY WORK IN ONE OR MORE OF THE FOLLOWING DEPARTMENTS: RESTAURANT, PUB, SPORTS, RECEPTION OR SOUVENIR SHOP. WE ARE LOOKING FOR FRIENDLY, OUTGOING INDIVIDUALS WHO WILL INTERACT WITH OUR GUESTS. OUR RESORT IS SITUATED IN THE HEART OF THE JAPANESE COUNTRYSIDE.

18–30

speaking **8 Work in pairs. Find out which of these jobs your partner would most like to do and why.**

writing **9 Choose one of the jobs and prepare an application for it. Adapt your CV to make it relevant to the job and then write a covering letter.**

speaking ## Job interviews

10 Translate these common interview questions into your own language. Use the advice below to help you.

Interviewer questions

Why would you like to work here?

Do you have experience of this type of work?

What skills and experience could you bring to the job?

How well do you work with other people?

Could you tell me why you left your last job?

What are your plans for the future?

Who could we contact for a reference?

Could you tell me about your hobbies and interests?

Candidate questions

Could you tell me more about the job?

Is there a dress code?

Who would I be working with?

Professional practice Translation

- listen to the whole message carefully before you start translating

- the level of formality and politeness depends on the relationship between the speaker or writer and the listener or reader

- use standard structures and phrases appropriate to the required register

- check that the register is consistent in your translation

11 Work in pairs. Exchange job applications. Prepare to interview your partner for the job he / she has chosen.

1 Read the relevant advertisement carefully.

2 Think what experience and qualities would be useful for the job.

3 Prepare a list of questions to ask the candidate.

4 Now read your partner's CV and covering letter.

5 Make notes and prepare questions about the CV.

12 Now interview your partner.

1 Greet the applicant and introduce yourself.

2 Ask the questions you have prepared.

3 Take notes and show an interest in the applicant's answers.

4 Invite the applicant to ask questions.

5 Thank the applicant and say when you will be in touch.

The great outdoors

vocabulary

1 What kind of tourist activities are possible with the following geographical features?

mountains	rivers	beaches	lakes	deserts	rainforests	glaciers

reading

2 Read the travel guide extract opposite. Are these statements true or false? Correct any false statements.

1 New Zealand is south of Australia.
2 The population of New Zealand is similar to that of the UK.
3 The North Island has a larger population than the South Island.
4 Auckland is the capital of New Zealand.
5 The South Island is famous for its mountains.
6 It rains a lot on the west coast of the South Island.
7 New Zealand is famous for the variety of its scenery.
8 There are thirty national parks in New Zealand.

PRONUNCIATION TIP
We don't pronounce the *s* in *island*.

Milford Sound, New Zealand ▲

Putting New Zealand on the map: the North and South Islands

NEW ZEALAND LIES in the Pacific Ocean, 1,600 km to the east of Australia. It consists of two large islands and a number of smaller ones. It's similar in size to the United Kingdom but it only has a population of about 3.8 million people. Most of them live in the North Island and over one million in Auckland, which is the country's largest city. New Zealand's capital is Wellington.

The South Island is a little larger than the North Island and is famous for its Southern Alps. You might think you were in Switzerland, not New Zealand. The eastern side of the Alps is dry but the west coast has a lot of rainfall and magnificent forests, lakes, mountains and glaciers. Christchurch is the largest city in the South Island. It is smaller than Auckland but has good international travel links.

New Zealand's landscape

THE MAIN CHARACTERISTIC of the landscape is its diversity: mountains, lakes, rivers, beaches, hills, volcanoes, rainforests and fjords are all contained in quite a small area. From the volcanoes of Tongariro National Park to the cliffs of Fjordland, New Zealand's thirteen national parks contain an amazing range of scenery, beautiful walking tracks and various plants and animals that are not found in other parts of the world.

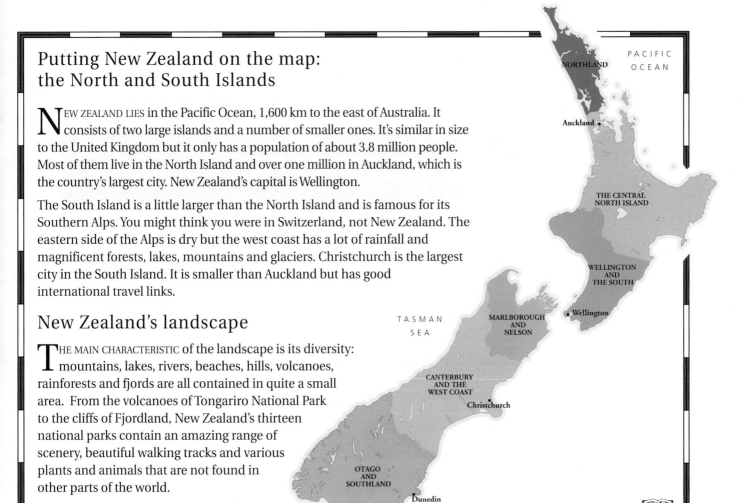

listening

3 Listen to the conversation between a tourist information officer and a tourist in New Zealand and answer the questions.

1 Which three 'star sights' are recommended?
2 What interesting fact is mentioned about the population of New Zealand?
3 What information does the tourist ask for?

4 Work in pairs. Student A, turn to page 119. Student B, turn to page 123. Use the tips to give your partner information about 'star sights' in your country.

Professional practice Selling tours

The following phrases are useful when selling tours.
- give some general information
  The scenery here is very spectacular / varied / dramatic.

- describe any local star sights
  It s the highest mountain / longest river ...

- give details about tours or excursions
  Would you like a map / information on excursions?

Changing a booking

5 Listen to the telephone conversation between Mr Gould and a travel agent and make the necessary changes to the booking form below.

Name:	Mr Stuart Gould
Tour title:	2-day Mount Cook National Park Tour
Number of pax:	14
Accommodation:	Mount Cook Motel
	7 double rooms
Departure date:	23 March, 8.20 am
Departure point:	Newmans Terminal, Christchurch

PTC0189-02

Pacific Travel Company

6 Listen again and answer the questions.

1 Why does Mr Gould want to change the booking?
2 What is he doing on 26 March?
3 What does Nathalie say about the coach service?

Language focus Present tenses as future

- We use the present simple for future timetables and schedules.
  *The coach **leaves** at 8.20 am.*
  *The museum **doesn't open** until 10 am.*
  *What time **does** the plane **land**?*

- We use the present continuous for future plans and personal arrangements.
  *We're **flying** to Auckland the following day.*
  *She's **not coming** with us on the tour.*
  ***Are** you **staying** overnight in the National Park?*

▶ For more information turn to page 129.

practice **7 Complete the sentences with the correct form of the present simple or the present continuous.**

1 The guided tour (*start*) ......*starts*........ in half an hour.
2 We (*take*) .... the bus to the airport tomorrow morning.
3 What time (*the Edinburgh train / leave*) ....?
4 They (*go on*) .... holiday in June this year.
5 When (*the hotel / close*) .... for the winter?
6 The next course (*start*) .... on 15th September and it (*not finish*) .... until February 21st.
7 When (*you / come*) .... to London again?
8 What (*she / do*) .... this summer?

8 Look at Mr Gould's postcard from his tour of Mount Cook and complete it using the present simple or present continuous.

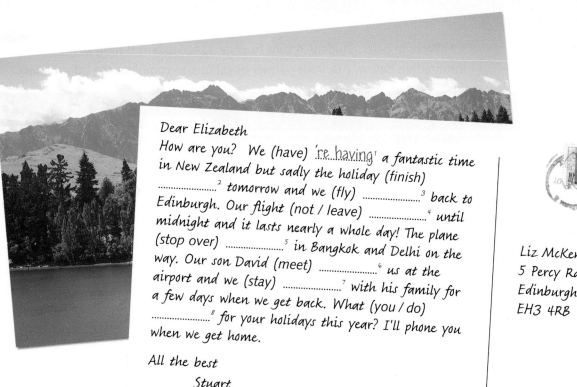

Dear Elizabeth

How are you? We (*have*) *'re having*[1] a fantastic time in New Zealand but sadly the holiday (*finish*) ....[2] tomorrow and we (*fly*) ....[3] back to Edinburgh. Our flight (*not / leave*) ....[4] until midnight and it lasts nearly a whole day! The plane (*stop over*) ....[5] in Bangkok and Delhi on the way. Our son David (*meet*) ....[6] us at the airport and we (*stay*) ....[7] with his family for a few days when we get back. What (*you / do*) ....[8] for your holidays this year? I'll phone you when we get home.

All the best
Stuart

Liz McKenzie
5 Percy Rd
Edinburgh
EH3 4RB

speaking **9 Work in groups. Find out about the other students' plans and arrangements for today, tomorrow, this weekend and their next holiday.**

	today	tomorrow	the weekend	next holiday
Student A	is working			
Student B				
Student C				

vocabulary Excursions

10 Match the pictures with the types of excursion.

bungee jumping | rafting   mountain biking
whale watching   hot-air ballooning

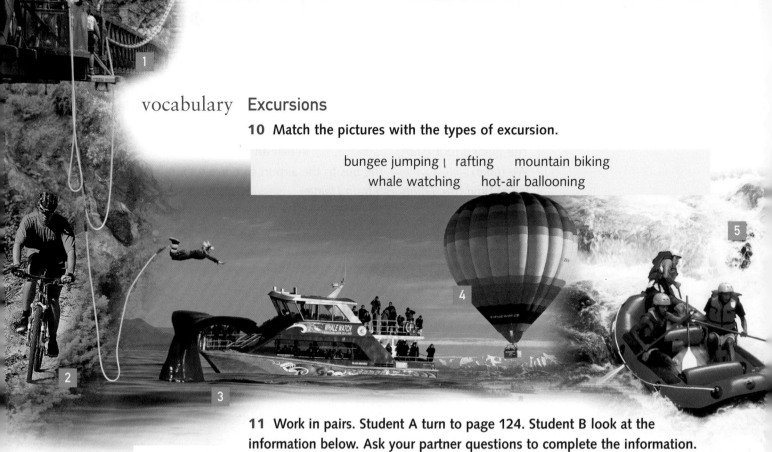

11 Work in pairs. Student A turn to page 124. Student B look at the information below. Ask your partner questions to complete the information.

WORLD BREAKS

Activities	Duration (days)	Price	Departure times
Whitewater rafting			
Nevis Whitewater	1	....	8.30 am & 1.30 pm
Kawarau River rafting	1	$199	....
Bungee jumping			
....	2 hours	$125	by individual arrangement
Skipper's Canyon	2 hours	....	by individual arrangement
Mountain biking			
Coronet Peak	....	From $125	–
....	2	....	–
Flightseeing			
Lake Wakatipu Tours	1	$339	8.45 am & 12.30 pm
Remarkable Mountains	1	$359	....

Valid 1 October 2002 – 30 September 2003
Note: Prices subject to change

12 Work in groups. Use the information on this page to design a five-day itinerary for a group of four young people.

Professional practice Confirming and checking

The following phrases are useful when checking and confirming information.

- repeat the important dates, times and prices
  Customer   *It s PTC0189-02.*
  Travel agent   *So that s PTC0189-02.*

- give yourself a little time to check information
  One moment, please.
  I ll just check that (for you).

- confirm bookings in writing
  I ll send you a fax / an email today to confirm those changes.

- check spellings and numbers that sound the same
  Is that P for Poland or D for Denmark?
  Sorry. Did you say fifty? Five-O?

listening

13 Listen to the telephone conversations and complete the information.

1 Reservation number: BGI 0271
2 Customer name: ....
3 Visa card number: ....
4 Reference number: ....
5 Email address: ....

pronunciation

Numbers and letters

14 Match the questions with the answers.

1 What's your email address?
2 What's your mobile phone number?
3 What's your date of birth?
4 How do you spell your surname?
5 What's your passport number?

a) It's 611 385 029.
b) It's S-P-R-I-N-G-F-I-E-L-D.
c) It's gloria.gomez@mtp.es.
d) It's VT064887350.
e) It's 21 February 1978.

Now work in pairs. Ask and answer the same questions.

speaking

Changing a booking

15 Work in pairs. Student A, you are the travel agent. Turn to page 119. Student B, you are a customer. Turn to page 123 and change your booking.

16 Write a fax / email confirming the changes to the booking and the new travel arrangements. Use the fax and email on pages 111–112 to help you.

Professional practice Confirming changes in writing

The following phrases are useful when confirming changes in writing.

With reference to your phone call today, ...
I / We are writing to confirm the changes to your booking.
The tour is for five days, departing from ... on ...
We hope you enjoy your tour with ...

Winter holidays

speaking **1** Look at the picture. What are the people doing? What other winter sports can you think of?

vocabulary **2** Match the pictures below with the words in the box.

> drag lift   chairlift   cable car   snowboard   skis   bindings   boots
> poles   goggles   helmet   gloves   ski jacket   ski pass

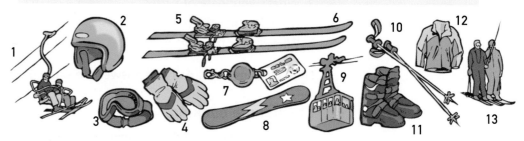

listening ## Ski resort jobs

3 Listen and match the speakers to the jobs. Would you like to do any of these jobs?

> ski instructor   chairlift attendant   ski hire shop assistant
> cafeteria staff   resort representative

4 Listen again and answer the questions.

1 What ski equipment is mentioned?
2 What should you do after you sit down on a chairlift?
3 What is the person learning to do in the skiing lesson?
4 Where is the entertainment?
5 What can you buy in the self-service area?

Language focus Giving instructions

We use imperatives to give instructions.

Put *your pass into the machine.*
Watch *me.*
Don't *bring wet skis into the hotel.*
Be *careful not to drop your ski poles.*

▶ For more information turn to page 130.

vocabulary **Giving directions**

5 Match the pictures to the directions in the box.

| go left   go right   go straight on   go upstairs   go downstairs |

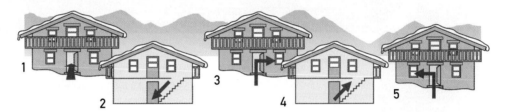

speaking **6 Work in pairs. Student A, turn to page 120. Student B, you work on reception at the ski lodge below. Use the expressions in the box above to give your partner directions. Then ask for directions to these places.**

| dining room   lounge   locker room   resort rep's office |

Reception

Ski hire

Main entrance

Car park

Locker room

Swimming pool ←

Bar

speaking

7 What special sporting events usually take place in your country? How does the city or area prepare for the event?

reading

8 Choose the best title for the online article. Give reasons for your choice.

1 No hotel rooms for Winter Games
2 New hotels in Salt Lake City
3 Overbooking for Winter Games

Salt Lake City (AP)

It's a little late to look for hotel rooms for the Winter Games in February in Salt Lake City, although the Salt Lake committee says rooms are available in Wendover, 113 miles west of Salt Lake City, and in other places outside the Salt Lake area.

Most Olympic visitors will stay in private homes and condominiums in the metropolitan area. Jerry Healey from Denver has sent a check for two rooms to a Salt Lake City owner for $550 per night. 'And I don't even know what it's going to be like,' Healey said.

SLOC, the Salt Lake Organizing Committee, has about 20,000 hotel rooms within two hours of Salt Lake City under contract. Sixty percent of these rooms are already booked by journalists, Olympic sponsors and officials.

Some rooms are reserved especially for guests who are staying a certain number of nights or buying Olympic packages that include lodging. Other rooms are held by hotels who will probably charge higher prices just before the Olympics.

As most of the city's hotel rooms were booked some time ago, SLOC is marketing private homes and condominiums for rental during the Olympics. Private residences cost from $150 to more than $3,000 per night. Condominiums run from $200 to about $550 per night.

Meanwhile, some Olympic visitors have already booked hotel rooms outside Salt Lake. 'I didn't think that people would want to stay here during the games,' said Sally East, owner of Larsen House Bed & Breakfast. 'I tell people that we are 100 miles away from Salt Lake City but they don't care. They just want to know if there is a good road to the sites and if it is open year-round.'

US / UK English

a condominium = a flat
a check = a cheque
a check = a bill
to run = to cost

9 Read the text again. Are these statements true or false? Correct any false statements.

1 It is easy to find rooms in Salt Lake City for the Olympic Winter Games.
2 SLOC says there are still rooms available in the Salt Lake area.
3 Most visitors will stay in private homes or apartments.
4 There are about 8,000 hotel rooms for journalists and Olympic officials.
5 Rates for private homes and condominiums are cheap.
6 Olympic visitors are prepared to drive long distances to the games.

Language focus The passive

- We make the passive by using the verb *be* + the past participle.
  *Most of the city s hotel rooms **were booked** some time ago.*

- We often use the passive for describing processes.
  *Some rooms **are reserved** for guests who are buying Olympic packages.*

- We use *by* to show the person or thing that does the action.
  *Many of these rooms are already booked **by** journalists and officials.*

▶ For more information turn to page 130.

practice **10** **Complete the text with the present or past form of the passive.**

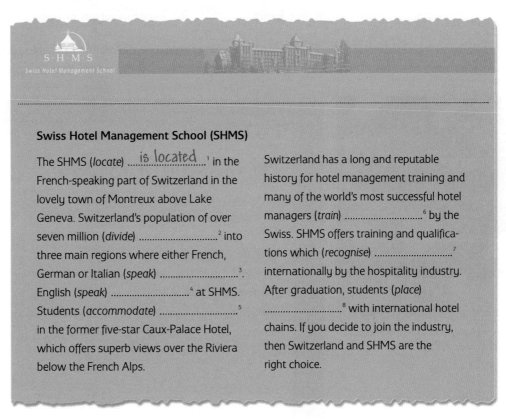

Swiss Hotel Management School (SHMS)

The SHMS (*locate*) ....*is located*....[1] in the French-speaking part of Switzerland in the lovely town of Montreux above Lake Geneva. Switzerland's population of over seven million (*divide*) ....[2] into three main regions where either French, German or Italian (*speak*) ....[3]. English (*speak*) ....[4] at SHMS. Students (*accommodate*) ....[5] in the former five-star Caux-Palace Hotel, which offers superb views over the Riviera below the French Alps.

Switzerland has a long and reputable history for hotel management training and many of the world's most successful hotel managers (*train*) ....[6] by the Swiss. SHMS offers training and qualifications which (*recognise*) ....[7] internationally by the hospitality industry. After graduation, students (*place*) ....[8] with international hotel chains. If you decide to join the industry, then Switzerland and SHMS are the right choice.

pronunciation ## The /ð/ and /θ/ sounds

11 Listen to the pronunciation of *th* in these words. Which words have the /ð/ sound (*the*) and which have the /θ/ sound (*think*)?

> this thanks thing weather thirty clothes fifth there

speaking **12 Work in groups. Imagine the Olympic Games are going to be held in your country. How would you plan for the following?**

> choosing the best city   accommodation special preparations   transport

13 What entertainment and activities do hotels and tour companies usually organise for holidaymakers at a winter holiday resort?

vocabulary **Entertainment**

14 Match these words with their definitions.

1 demonstration   a) entertainment at a theatre or on television
2 exhibition   b) explanation to show how to use or do something
3 show   c) musical group that are playing in public
4 arts and crafts   d) game of questions to find out who knows the most
5 race   e) products made by hand
6 competition   f) game to see who is the fastest
7 quiz   g) public display of products or works of art
8 live band   h) event in which people try to be the best at something

listening **15** Melanie is a resort representative for Inghams, a UK tour operator. Listen to her describe the holiday entertainment and complete the programme.

▲ An Inghams resort representative

PROGRAMME OF EVENTS

	morning	afternoon	evening
Sunday	–	–	Welcome meeting ₁
Monday	Ski school	....................²	–
Tuesday	....................³	Children's race	–
Wednesday	Ski school	....................⁴	–
Thursday	Ski school	Beginners' race	....................⁵
Friday	Ski school	–	....................⁶

Events and times are subject to change.

16 Listen again and answer the questions.

1 Where is the welcome meeting?
2 On what condition can children go cross-country skiing?
3 What is 'snowshoeing'?
4 Where is the demonstration of new ski equipment?
5 Who can take part in the torchlit descent of the mountain?
6 What is organised for the farewell party?
7 Where should people sign up for the activities?

Professional practice Selling optional extras

The following phrases are useful when selling optional extras.

- always be enthusiastic
  It's lots of fun.

- explain what is included
  We'll organise the hire equipment.
  We'll provide the transport from the hotel at 6 pm.

- show interest in the customers needs
  You don't have to be a skier to take part.
  Children can come along.

- explain what the benefits are
  We're offering lots of super prizes.

speaking **17 Work in groups. You are a rival representative in the same resort as Melanie. Design a seven-day entertainment programme to win customers from Melanie. Prepare your programme and then present it to the group.**

writing **18 You receive this email from a tour operator. Write back giving details of your entertainment programme and prices. Use the email on page 112 to help you.**

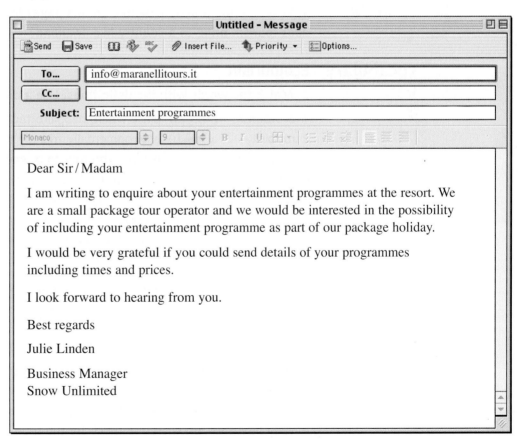

Dear Sir / Madam

I am writing to enquire about your entertainment programmes at the resort. We are a small package tour operator and we would be interested in the possibility of including your entertainment programme as part of our package holiday.

I would be very grateful if you could send details of your programmes including times and prices.

I look forward to hearing from you.

Best regards

Julie Linden

Business Manager
Snow Unlimited

13

Land of smiles

speaking **1** What are the tourist activities on this page? What benefits and problems does tourism bring to a country like Thailand?

vocabulary **Ecotourism**

2 Match the words with the definitions. Use a dictionary to help you.

1 ecotourism   a) place where people often go for holidays
2 rubbish   b) environmentally-friendly tourism
3 expedition   c) person who tries to protect the environment
4 conservationist d) long journey to a dangerous place
5 resort   e) thick tropical forest with a lot of vegetation
6 ecosystem   f) things that have been thrown away
7 environment   g) how all plants and animals relate to each other
8 jungle   h) the conditions that plants and animals live in

reading **3** Read the text on the opposite page and decide where it came from.

a) newspaper or magazine   b) holiday brochure   c) guidebook on Thailand

4 Now read the text in detail and answer these questions.

1 What damage does mass jungle trekking do to the environment?
2 What pollution problem does Meeya Hawa mention?
3 How is the Kiriwong Club trying to protect the environment?
4 Why does the club charge so much for the four-day trek?
5 Why do you think TAT wants the Kiriwong Club to drop the price?
6 Who does Nipat Boonpet think is responsible for the damage?

ECOTOURISM IN THAILAND

Tour companies in Thailand advertise jungle treks, scuba diving and other expeditions as 'nature tourism'. But the popularity of these activities has caused environmental problems. Like mass tourism, mass jungle trekking can damage the ecosystem and the living and working conditions of local people.

As a solution to the problem, the Tourism Authority of Thailand (TAT) introduced the idea of ecotourism here a few years ago. Ecotourism is tourism that is environmentally friendly and that also benefits local communities.

Meeya Hawa is a local conservation worker in the fishing village of Jao Mai. He explained some of the problems. 'When the tourists come, they stay at comfortable resort hotels and ignore our small huts. They go to the island by the resort's boats and eat at the resort's restaurant. And they throw rubbish into the sea.'

But things are changing. In the mountain village of Kiriwong, the villagers have started an Ecotourism Club with rules to protect the environment. The club has limited the number of mountain trekkers to only thirty a month. Each trekker pays about 3000 baht (750 US dollars) for a four-day trek which includes food, accommodation, sightseeing and a donation to the community.

Many tourists complain and say the mountain should be for everyone. The director of TAT in the area also thinks Kiriwong should lower the price to attract tourists but the club doesn't agree. Nipat Boonpet, the club's secretary, says, 'Tourists only think of what they pay for food, travelling and accommodation. Nature for them is free. It is not.'

It now seems that if there isn't a real change in the thinking of both tour operators and tourists, the natural environment will be destroyed.

Adapted from *Tourism Principles and Practice*, Longman 1998.

vocabulary **5 Complete the table with words from the text.**

verb	noun	verb	noun
damage [1]	damage	.... [5]	protection
solve	.... [2]	donate	.... [6]
.... [3]	benefit	.... [7]	attraction
conserve	.... [4]	.... [8]	destruction

speaking **6 Work in groups. Discuss these questions.**

- How do tourists damage the environment in your country or region?
- What types of ecotourism are there in your country or region?
- Do tourists have to pay a fee to enter national parks and other green areas?
- Do you think nature should be free for everyone?

KEEP CLEAN
KEEP NATURE PLEASE
AO PRAO RESORT
KOH SAMED

7 Work in pairs. Read these statements about Thai culture. Discuss whether you think they are true or false. Then read the text below to find out.

1 Thais are very friendly people.
2 People in Thailand like to argue passionately.
3 There are many different types of greeting (*Wai*) in Thailand.
4 Foreigners shouldn't use the *Wai* greeting.
5 Thai children are greeted with a pat on the head.
6 Women shouldn't sit next to monks.
7 The monks are part of a very small religious order in Thailand.
8 You have to wear special shoes when visiting Thai temples.

Etiquette

THAILAND is often called 'the land of smiles'. The Thais, who are very friendly and helpful, are easy to get on with. They are very tolerant and will try to avoid arguments and public confrontation.

GREETING PEOPLE

THE THAI GREETING, which is known as the *Wai*, consists of putting your palms together and lifting them towards your chin. The *Wai* comes from an ancient greeting that used to show that people were not carrying weapons. The type of *Wai* you do depends on your class, age and gender. If you're a foreigner and you're not sure what to do, just copy the person who is greeting you. You shouldn't *Wai* children or workers such as waiters.

BODY LANGUAGE

NEVER TOUCH someone's head, which is the most sacred part of the body for Thais, not even a child's. Thais think the feet are the lowliest part of the body, so you should never point your feet towards someone or put them on a table. When you visit a temple, you have to kneel with your feet facing away from the Buddha which is a sacred image.

MONKS

MONKHOOD is a very respected institution. It is the next most important part of Thai society after royalty. There are some taboos when dealing with monks. For example, a monk mustn't touch a woman or receive anything directly from her. When travelling on public transport, women should not sit next to or near a monk. Most teenage boys become monks for a few months, which is seen as lucky for their families.

TEMPLES

YOU SHOULD take off your shoes when you enter a temple or *wat*. There are some areas of temples that women cannot visit.

DK

Language focus Defining relative pronouns

Look at the examples and complete the information below.

Songkran *is a Thai festival* **which / that** *celebrates the Buddhist New Year.*
A monk is a man **who / that** *performs religious ceremonies.*

- We use <u>which</u> , ... or .... for defining things and people.
- We use .... or .... for objects and .... or .... for people.

practice   **8 Match these sentence halves.**

1 You should not *Wai* workers ...   a) which cover upper arms and legs.
2 The person who is lower in social status ...   b) who are waiters or street sellers.
3 Foreigners who show impatience ...   c) has to hold the *Wai* for longer.
4 You can't take photos of sacred sights ...   d) which are connected to royalty.
5 On temple visits you must wear clothes ...   e) will be ignored by Thai waiters.

Language focus Non-defining relative pronouns

- We also use *which* or *who* when we want to give extra information.
- The extra information is shown between commas.

The New Year, **which** *is an international festival, is celebrated in April.*
The Thais, **who** *are Buddhists, celebrate many different festivals.*

▶ For more information turn to page 130.

9 Underline the defining and non-defining pronouns in these sentences and add any necessary commas.

1 The *Wai*, <u>which</u> is the traditional greeting, involves putting your palms together. non-defining
2 It is illegal to criticise the Royal Family which is the most important institution in Thailand.
3 Foreigners who are used to quick service in restaurants shouldn't show impatience or they will be ignored by waiters.
4 Monks who never return the *Wai* greeting are very respected in Thailand.
5 Never step on a temple threshold as Thais believe that one of the nine spirits that inhabit a building lives in the threshold.
6 The Thai national anthem which is played twice a day in public parks and buildings is also played before cinema performances.

speaking   **10 What kind of etiquette and customs are there in your country? Think about the following.**

greeting people   body language   dress code   communicating

A holiday in Thailand

PROFESSIONAL TIPS
• be well-informed about what you are selling
• advise the customer of all options
• make a recommendation

11 Listen to Anne-Marie booking a holiday in Thailand. What does her travel agent try to sell her? Is the travel agent good at selling?

12 Listen again and answer the questions.
1 What kind of insurance does the travel agent recommend?
2 Why is it better than the customer's own insurance company's cover?
3 What does the package include?
4 When would any medical costs be paid?
5 What else does the insurance include?
6 How much does the insurance cost?

vocabulary **Medical equipment**

13 Look at Anne-Marie's medical kit and label the items with the words in the box. When would you need to use these items?

| scissors tweezers plasters thermometer mosquito repellent |
| aspirin bandage antiseptic cream sunblock pocketknife |

14 You are going trekking for three days in northern Thailand. What clothes and equipment would you take with you? Make a packing list.

'TREKKING THREE DAYS / TWO NIGHTS ON THE TOP OF THAILAND. EXPLORE THAILAND'S HIGHEST MOUNTAIN, DOI INTHANON. ENJOY SPECTACULAR FORESTS AND REFRESHING WATERFALLS. STAY OVERNIGHT IN LOCAL HILL TRIBE VILLAGES.

listening **15** Now listen to a local guide telling a group of trekkers what to pack. How many items on your list do you hear? Add any other items to your packing list.

16 Listen again and answer the questions.

1 What kind of places are they going to visit?

2 What kind of weather and temperatures are they going to have?

3 What dangers are there going to be?

vocabulary **17 Match the US English with the UK English words.**

US English

1 flashlight

2 pants

3 running shoes

4 rainjacket

5 jogging suit

UK English

a) trainers

b) torch

c) tracksuit

d) trousers

e) anorak

Professional practice Giving health advice

The following phrases are useful when giving health advice.

It's **wise / best to** avoid uncooked food.

I recommend you use insect repellent.

It's essential / advisable to take malaria pills.

Make sure you drink lots of fluids when it is hot.

Avoid walk**ing / You shouldn't** walk around in the midday sun.

Pack an anorak **in case** it rains.

speaking **18 Work in pairs. Student A, turn to page 121. Student B, look at the safety advice below and answer your partner's questions.**

▲ *Tiger Balm - Asia's miracle cure for all headaches, muscle pains and insect bites.*

Travelling in Thailand

Thailand is a safe country for travellers but some simple precautions are still required. Hotels and taxis are safe and it is safe for women travellers. If travelling alone, keep in touch with someone on a regular basis. There are plenty of well-stocked pharmacies that sell insect repellents and basic medicines. Heat and humidity can be a problem so drink lots of fluids, avoid the midday sun and take plenty of rest.

Diarrhoea is a common complaint. If it occurs, eat plain food for a few days and drink lots of fluids. Avoid tap water – bottled water is easily available – and avoid crushed ice in drinks from street vendors.

Now ask your partner for advice for travelling to South Africa. Ask about:

personal safety   common health problems for travellers
driving in South Africa   safety on safari

writing **19 Prepare a short information leaflet for travellers to your country or area.**

Enjoy your stay

speaking   **1 Look at the hotel bill. What extra costs are usually added to a hotel bill?**

The
Admiral Hotel

Bed and buffet breakfast 3 nights @ 2650	7950
Room service	235
Minibar	47
Telephone calls	1740
Registration fee	87
Tax (7%)	704
Total	RUR 10763

5% sales tax when paying by credit card
Thank you for choosing The Admiral Hotel. We hope you enjoyed your stay.

listening   **Checking out**

2 Listen to Mr Collins check out of the Admiral Hotel in St Petersburg. How does he react to the bill? Why?

3 Listen again and answer the questions.

1 What did Mr Collins order from room service?
2 Where is the information about prices?
3 Who did Mr Collins telephone?
4 Why are the phone calls from the hotel expensive?
5 What is the correct total amount for the bill?
6 How is he going to pay the bill?

vocabulary **Currencies**

4 Match the abbreviations to the currencies and countries.

1 RUR	pound	Russia
2 USD	rouble	Eurozone countries
3 THB	peso	Mexico
4 NZD	baht	the UK
5 EUR	rand	Poland
6 GBP	zloty	New Zealand
7 MXN	dollar	the USA
8 PLN	Euro	Thailand
9 ZAR	dollar	South Africa

To avoid confusion always use the international three-letter abbreviations for currencies. The letters come before the amount.

pronunciation **Numbers**

5 Listen and practise saying these numbers from the bill.

235   704   1,740   7,950   10,763

Professional practice Preparing bills

The following checklist is useful when preparing bills.
- avoid hidden extras — guests are not happy if they feel overcharged
- display an up-to-date price list at all times
- include any extra costs and taxes on price lists
- deal with bill queries politely and efficiently
- remember that guests can easily forget what services they have used
  I'll just check our records. It says here there was a call yesterday evening.
- stay calm, apologise and offer to correct mistakes immediately
  Oh yes, I do apologise, we have made a mistake here. That should be ...

---

speaking **6 Work in pairs. Student A, you are the receptionist at the Admiral Hotel. Look at the bill, turn to page 123 and answer the guest's questions. Student B, you are the guest. Turn to page 121.**

The Admiral Hotel

02/765
Room number 233

Bed and buffet breakfast 2 nights @ 2650	5300
Car park fee	180
Minibar	34
Registration fee	87
Check-out	56
Tax (7%)	396
Total	RUR 6053

vocabulary **Checking in**

7 Match the words or phrases with their definitions. Use a dictionary to help you.

1 upgrade   a) fixed cost that does not change
2 upsell   b) improve the category of something
3 guest registration   c) check-in
4 available   d) worth or price of something
5 availability   e) special price offered to businesses
6 corporate rate   f) free or vacant
7 value   g) number of rooms that are free
8 flat charge   h) convince a client to purchase an upgraded service

reading **8 Read the webpage below and answer the questions.**

1 What happens if the best rooms in a hotel are vacant?
2 Why do guests not know that better rooms are vacant?
3 Why do guests sometimes need a better type of room?
4 How can you convince a guest to book a better room at check-in?
5 What's another way of describing a reduced price for companies?

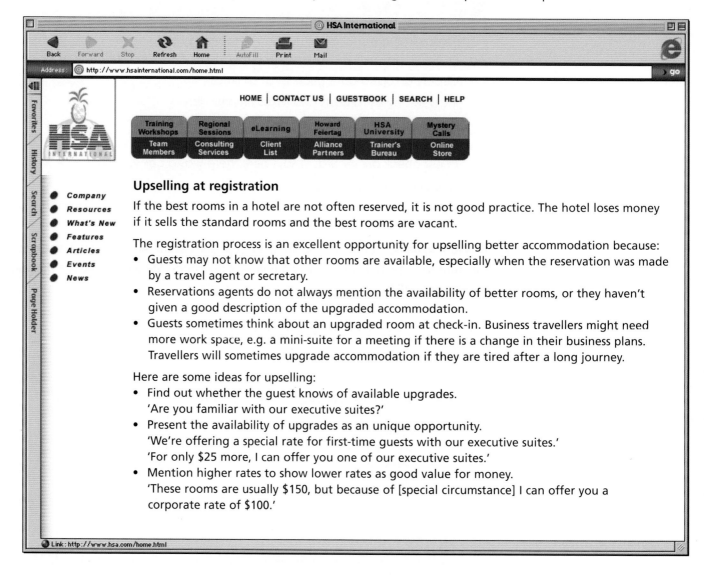

HOME | CONTACT US | GUESTBOOK | SEARCH | HELP

Training Workshops | Regional Sessions | eLearning | Howard Feiertag | HSA University | Mystery Calls
Team Members | Consulting Services | Client List | Alliance Partners | Trainer's Bureau | Online Store

- Company
- Resources
- What's New
- Features
- Articles
- Events
- News

Upselling at registration

If the best rooms in a hotel are not often reserved, it is not good practice. The hotel loses money if it sells the standard rooms and the best rooms are vacant.

The registration process is an excellent opportunity for upselling better accommodation because:
- Guests may not know that other rooms are available, especially when the reservation was made by a travel agent or secretary.
- Reservations agents do not always mention the availability of better rooms, or they haven't given a good description of the upgraded accommodation.
- Guests sometimes think about an upgraded room at check-in. Business travellers might need more work space, e.g. a mini-suite for a meeting if there is a change in their business plans. Travellers will sometimes upgrade accommodation if they are tired after a long journey.

Here are some ideas for upselling:
- Find out whether the guest knows of available upgrades.
  'Are you familiar with our executive suites?'
- Present the availability of upgrades as an unique opportunity.
  'We're offering a special rate for first-time guests with our executive suites.'
  'For only $25 more, I can offer you one of our executive suites.'
- Mention higher rates to show lower rates as good value for money.
  'These rooms are usually $150, but because of [special circumstance] I can offer you a corporate rate of $100.'

Language focus Conditional 1

- We use the following form for results that always follow an action
  If + present simple + present simple
  If we **sell** standard rooms and the best rooms are vacant, we **lose** money.

- We use the following form for predicting results of future actions
  If + present simple + modal verb + infinitive
  Mr Johnson **will be** very happy *if* he **gets** an upgrade.

- We can change the order of the two parts of the sentence
  If travellers **are** tired, they **will** often **upgrade** accommodation. (with comma)
  Travellers **will** often **upgrade** accommodation *if* they **are** tired. (no comma)

▶ For more information turn to page 130.

practice   **9 Complete the webpage with the correct form of the verbs in brackets.**

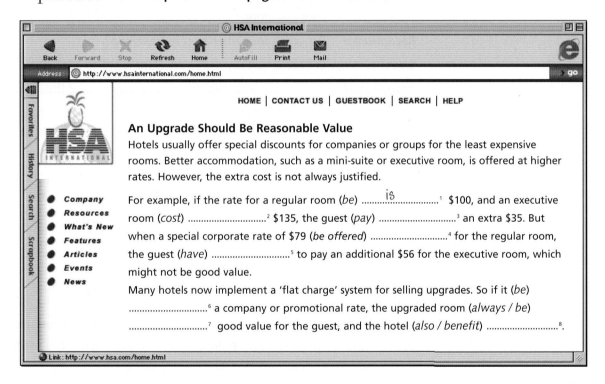

10 Use the webpage to make conditional sentences.

If we…
upsell at registration
guests upgrade rooms
guests be happier
guests re-book
the hotel make more money
staff earn commission

If we upsell at registration, guests will upgrade rooms.
....
....
....
....

speaking   **11 Work in pairs. Student A, you are the receptionist at the Admiral Hotel in St Petersburg. Turn to page 122. Student B, you are a guest. Turn to page 124.**

12 Listen to Ms Reed check out of the Admiral Hotel and answer the questions.

1 How does the receptionist start the upselling process?
2 What does he try to sell?
3 How does he 'sell' its benefits?
4 Does the receptionist complete the booking?
5 What upgrade does he try to sell?
6 What further hotel service does he offer?

13 Listen again and complete the phrases the receptionist uses when he re-books the guest.

Guest	I'll ask my PA to book a room when I get back to the office.
Receptionist	If you like, *I could book it for you* ₁ now. It won't take a minute.
Receptionist	Do you know when you're travelling?
Guest	Let me check my diary. Yes, June 14th to 18th.
Receptionist	..........................² four nights, ...³ the 18th?
Receptionist	Oh good, we still have our mini-suites. ....⁴ more, I can book you a mini-suite. I'm sure ....⁵ more comfortable for meetings.
Receptionist	Here's a programme. You can fax me and our concierge ....⁶ book them for you.
Guest	Oh, right. That's great. Thanks for everything.
Receptionist	....⁷ . We look forward to seeing you in June Ms Reed.

Polite intonation

We use *shall* and the first person for making polite offers and suggestions.
***Shall I** book you a mini-suite?*
***Shall I** help you with your bags, sir?*

14 Listen to how the voice goes up and down in these questions to make them sound enthusiastic and polite. Then practise saying the sentences.

1 Are you planning to visit St Petersburg again, madam?
2 Do you know there's a festival on in June, madam?
3 Do you know when you're travelling?
4 Would you like me to book you a room now?
5 Shall I book you into a suite on your next visit?
6 Did you know we offer special rates to companies?
7 Have you seen our weekend offer?

practice   **15 Complete the memo about booking return reservations with the correct form of the verbs in brackets.**

> To: All reception desk staff   MEMO
> Re: Re-booking guests
>
> ___
>
> Booking return reservations at check-out is especially important for us as so many of our guests are business travellers who return on a monthly or weekly basis. If this sales opportunity (*be*) ....is........¹ missed, guests might decide to try the competition next time, or they (*be*) ....² forced to stay in another hotel.
>
> At present, when departing guests (*ask*) ....³ about return reservations, most (*be given*) ....⁴ the hotel's phone number or a central reservations number. If front-desk salespeople (*invite*) ....⁵ departing guests to return, the guest (*book*) ....⁶ their next stay on the spot. Please ensure that in future all guests are invited to book their next reservation at check-out.

Professional practice Front-desk staff in sales

Front-desk staff can also take responsibility for sales. Look at the tapescript for exercise 12 on page 142 and find phrases for the following.

• upsell at check-out

  ....

• re-book guests at check-out

  ....

• point out the value of the room rate

  ....

• offer information about hotel facilities and services to guests

  ....

speaking   **16 Work in pairs. Role-play a check-out situation. Student A, turn to page 122. Student B, you are a hotel receptionist. Use these tips, remember to upsell at check-out and try to re-book the guest.**

• Check out the guest. Make sure you mention any additional charges.
• Tell the guest about any future festivals or events and try to re-book them to an upgraded room. If they book a mini-suite, you will get higher commission.
• Say goodbye to the guest in a polite and friendly way.

Winds of change

speaking **Climate**

1 **When do the seasons begin and end in your country and what's the best time of year to visit?**

reading **2** **Look at the information on the opposite page and answer these questions.**

1 Where does it rain the most in Mexico?
2 Which is the coldest place in Mexico in winter?
3 Where is the sunniest place in winter?
4 Which place has most rain in January?
5 Where is it warm all year round?
6 What landscape can you find in the yellow regions?

vocabulary **The weather forecast**

3 **Match the weather symbols with the words.**

> heavy rain I showers   sunshine   strong winds
> snow   cloudy / overcast

4 **Match the words with their definitions. Use a dictionary to help you.**

1 hurricane   a) sudden bright light in the sky during a storm
2 thunder   b) very strong, violent wind
3 lightning   c) sudden loud noise in the sky during a storm
4 flood   d) amount of water in the air
5 frost   e) rain that lasts for a short time
6 shower   f) large amount of water covering land
7 humidity   g) result of the temperature falling below 0°C

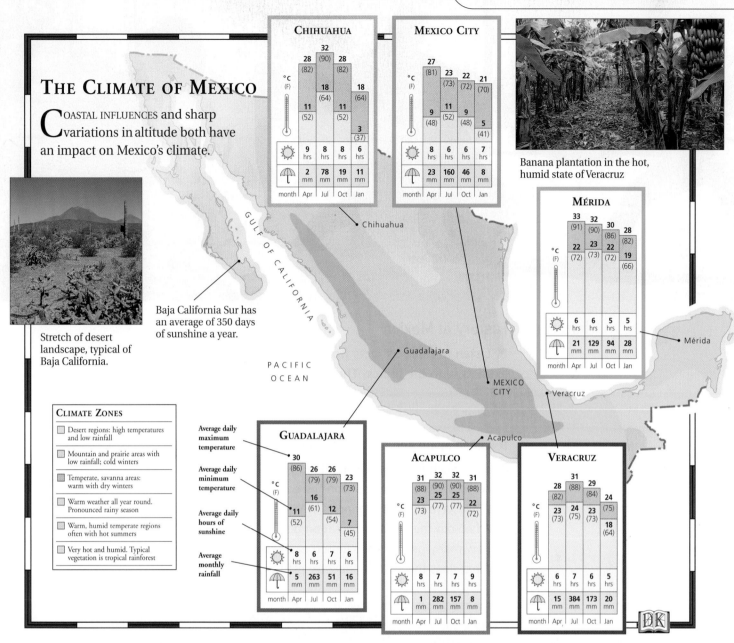

THE CLIMATE OF MEXICO

Coastal influences and sharp variations in altitude both have an impact on Mexico's climate.

Banana plantation in the hot, humid state of Veracruz

Stretch of desert landscape, typical of Baja California.

Baja California Sur has an average of 350 days of sunshine a year.

CLIMATE ZONES
- Desert regions: high temperatures and low rainfall
- Mountain and prairie areas with low rainfall; cold winters
- Temperate, savanna areas: warm with dry winters
- Warm weather all year round. Pronounced rainy season
- Warm, humid temperate regions often with hot summers
- Very hot and humid. Typical vegetation is tropical rainforest

speaking **5** Work in pairs. Student A, choose a town or region in Mexico. Student B, ask *Yes / No* questions to guess which town or region Student A is thinking of.

Professional practice Describing the weather

The following phrases are useful when describing weather conditions.

It gets very humid in summer here.
It rains a lot here in springtime.
It's hot for the time of year.
The weather forecast said there may be a storm later today.
It's best to take a coat because it gets cold at night.

listening **6** Listen to today's forecast for Mexico and mark the weather on the map. Which is the best and the worst place to be? Why?

webtask **7** What is the weather forecast for your area tomorrow?

listening **History of Mexico**

8 Listen to three extracts from a TV programme about Mexico. Match the extracts with the topics. There is one extra topic.

> history   entertainment   landscape   economy

9 Listen again and answer the questions.

1 How much of Mexico is arid land?
2 What is the landscape like in the south?
3 What were the Maya experts in?
4 When did the Mayan civilisation disappear?
5 How many people visit Mexico each year?
6 What does the tourism industry plan to do?

Language focus   Tense review 1: Present and past forms

Match the examples with the rules.

- Present simple
  1 *Over half of Mexico's land **has** very little rainfall each year.*
  2 *Over one and a half million US visitors **go** to Mexico each year.*

- Present continuous
  3 *Tourism **is growing** very quickly in Mexico.*

- Present perfect
  4 *Archaeologists **have studied** the Mayan civilisation for many years.*

- Past simple
  5 *Mexico **received** over twenty million tourists last year.*

a) facts that are true and do not change
b) events that started in the past and are still happening now
c) temporary, changing or developing situations
d) events that happen regularly
e) finished events

practice **10 Complete the sentences about Mexico using the correct present or past tense of the verbs in brackets. Some verbs are in the passive.**

1 Mexico (*be*) ....was.......... a Spanish colony for 300 years.

2 Independence Day (*celebrate*) .... on 16 September.

3 The Aztec pyramids (*use*) .... for human sacrifices.

4 Many new bars (*open*) .... in downtown Mexico City in recent years.

5 Central and southern Mexico (*often visit*) .... for their Mayan ruins.

6 Mariachi bands can (*see*) .... in the Plaza Garibaldi in Mexico City, playing songs about love.

7 The National Anthropological Museum (*be*) .... open since 1964.

Language focus Tense review 2: Future forms

- Present simple for schedules and timetables
  *The museum **isn't** open next Monday.*

- Present continuous for personal plans and arrangements
  *We**'re flying** to Cancún next week.*

- Going to for personal intentions or predictions with evidence
  *We**'re going to visit** the Mayan ruins.*
  *The tourism industry **is going to expand.***

- Will for predictions or offers
  *On the south coast it **will** also **be** extremely hot.*
  *I**'ll fax** you the information on Acapulco.*

---

11 Complete the brochure extract with the correct present, past or future forms of the verbs in brackets.

The ways to celebrate a marriage (change) have changed.¹ along with the changes in the travel industry. In the past, couples typically (not / go) ....² abroad for a honeymoon. Today's honeymooners are looking for something exotic and romantic. The trend in recent years (be) ....³ back to traditional weddings associated with earlier generations. But couples nowadays (want) ....⁴ a different honeymoon experience and they are going further away for their honeymoons.

Another trend is that more couples (go) ....⁵ abroad to get married on their honeymoon. This holiday package (be) ....⁶ a popular concept in the Caribbean and Mexico for many years. The all-inclusive honeymoon trip is another package that (start) ....⁷ in Jamaica. This 'one price pays for everything' trip is convenient for families who (buy) ....⁸ a honeymoon package for the couple as a wedding present.

One thing that (not / change) ....⁹ is that people will spend more money on a honeymoon than on a regular holiday, which (continue) ....¹⁰ to make honeymoons an important sector of tourism in the future.

12 Match the tourists with the type of tourism in the box.

| mass tourism | business travel | ecotourism |

13 Now listen to three tourists talk about Mexico and answer the questions.

1 Who wants to do some water sports?
2 Who thinks restaurant service is not as good as in their country?
3 Who is really looking forward to their holiday?
4 Who likes shopping on holiday?
5 Who was bitten by insects?
6 Who did some sightseeing?

Which of the tourists talks about a) the present b) the past or c) the future? Which verb tenses do they use? Check the tapescript on page 143.

14 Work in pairs. Discuss the following questions.

• How has tourism changed your country in the last ten years?
• Which attractions or resorts did not exist ten years ago?
• Which areas are the most / least popular with tourists? Why?
• Which areas are protected from development? Why?
• What future plans for development are there for tourism in your country?

speaking   A tourism development project

15 Work in groups. Choose an area in your country that hasn't been developed yet for tourism. Use the information below to prepare a tourism development plan. Then present your plan to the class.

Adventure holidays ▲

tourist profile
age, nationality, interests, spending power

main resorts
towns or cities and their attractions

▲ Sports holidays

Tourism development plan

environmental protection
beaches, forests, culture

transport
airports, roads, rail

accommodation
types and availability

Mass tourism / beach holidays ▲

▲ Holidays in the country

Professional practice	Giving presentations (2)

The following phrases are useful when giving presentations.
* use visuals such as maps and charts to present your ideas
  This map / chart shows ...
  As you can see, there is / are ...

* present the development project in a positive way
  This is an exciting opportunity for ...
  The benefits of this plan include ...

* summarise the main points in your conclusion
  To summarise, we think that ...

* be prepared to answer questions about the project
  Does anyone have any questions?
  Would anyone like to ask a question?
  That's a good question. I think ...

Consolidation ③

Making arrangements

1 Complete the email with the present simple or continuous form of the verbs in brackets.

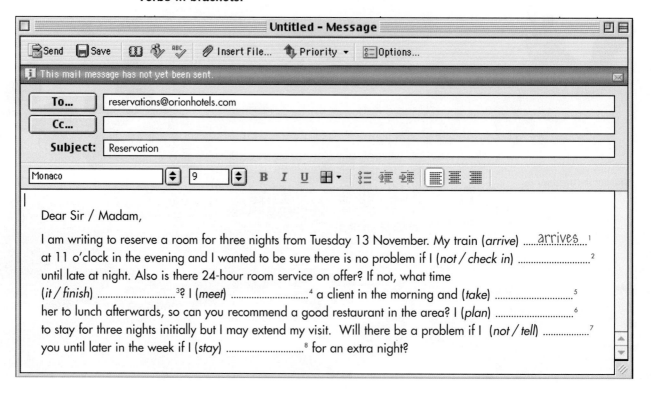

```
┌──────────────────────────────────────────────────────────────────────────┐
│ ▢ ░░░░░░░░░░░░░  Untitled – Message  ░░░░░░░░░░░░░░░░░░░░░░      ▢▢ ▢▢     │
├──────────────────────────────────────────────────────────────────────────┤
│ ⊠Send  ▢Save  ▢▢ ▢ ᴬᴮᶜ    ∅ Insert File...  ⬆ Priority ▾  ▢ Options...   │
├──────────────────────────────────────────────────────────────────────────┤
│ ⓘ This mail message has not yet been sent.                          ✉      │
├──────────────────────────────────────────────────────────────────────────┤
│  │ To... │  reservations@orionhotels.com                                  │
│  │ Cc... │                                                                │
│  Subject: │ Reservation                                                   │
├──────────────────────────────────────────────────────────────────────────┤
│  Monaco        ▢  │ 9 │▢  B  I  U  ▦▾  ▤ ▤ ▤  ▤ ▤ ▤                       │
├──────────────────────────────────────────────────────────────────────────┤
```

Dear Sir / Madam,

I am writing to reserve a room for three nights from Tuesday 13 November. My train (*arrive*) ......*arrives*...[1] at 11 o'clock in the evening and I wanted to be sure there is no problem if I (*not / check in*) ....[2] until late at night. Also is there 24-hour room service on offer? If not, what time (*it / finish*) ....[3]? I (*meet*) ....[4] a client in the morning and (*take*) ....[5] her to lunch afterwards, so can you recommend a good restaurant in the area? I (*plan*) ....[6] to stay for three nights initially but I may extend my visit. Will there be a problem if I (*not / tell*) ....[7] you until later in the week if I (*stay*) ....[8] for an extra night?

The passive

2 Complete the newspaper article with the present or past simple passive form of the verbs in brackets.

Reduce, Re-use, Recycle!

Water and energy-saving ideas (*promote*) *are promoted*[1] in many hotels nowadays. One hotel in Miami reported that their water bills (*reduce*) ....[2] enormously after they made simple toilet adaptations and special taps (*put*) ....[3] in. At the same time, shampoo and soap dispensers (*install*) ....[4] in all guests' rooms to save money. Here are some more examples of changes that the hotel has introduced. Public areas (*leave*) ....[5] unscented now and plants are used instead to keep the air fresh. The stationery that (*put*) ....[6] in guest rooms is on 100% recycled paper. The linen (*not / change*) ....[7] every day of the guest's stay but on request only. Similarly, guests (*ask*) ....[8] to complete a card when they want fresh towels. Hotel guests (*invite*) ....[9] by notices displayed in their rooms to participate in recycling. Last year the restaurant and bar areas (*redesign*) ....[10] to use only daylight for as much of the day as possible. The hotel manager says that these adaptations have saved the hotel a lot of money and the environmentally-friendly ideas are good for public relations.

Conditional 1

3 Complete these Russian superstitions with the correct form of the verbs in brackets.

1 If you (*leave*) ....leave....... something behind in Russia, it means you (*come*) .... back.

2 If you (*whistle*) .... indoors, you (*lose*) .... all your money.

3 If you (*light*) .... a cigarette from a candle, it (*bring*) .... you bad luck.

4 If you (*spill*) .... salt at the table you (*have*) .... bad luck unless you (*throw*) .... three pinches over your left shoulder.

speaking

4 Work in pairs. Student A turn to page 120. Student B turn to page 122. Look at the items and write definitions for your partner to guess the words.

translation

The Butternut Inn

5 Translate this webpage into your own language. Use a dictionary and the advice below to help you.

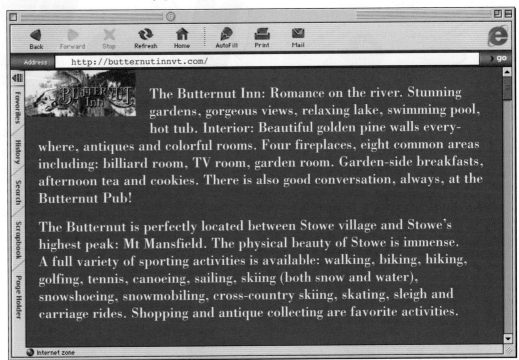

The Butternut Inn: Romance on the river. Stunning gardens, gorgeous views, relaxing lake, swimming pool, hot tub. Interior: Beautiful golden pine walls every-where, antiques and colorful rooms. Four fireplaces, eight common areas including: billiard room, TV room, garden room. Garden-side breakfasts, afternoon tea and cookies. There is also good conversation, always, at the Butternut Pub!

The Butternut is perfectly located between Stowe village and Stowe's highest peak: Mt Mansfield. The physical beauty of Stowe is immense. A full variety of sporting activities is available: walking, biking, hiking, golfing, tennis, canoeing, sailing, skiing (both snow and water), snowshoeing, snowmobiling, cross-country skiing, skating, sleigh and carriage rides. Shopping and antique collecting are favorite activities.

Professional practice **Translation**

- read the whole text carefully before you start translating
- read a similar text in your own language before you start
- think about the purpose of the text — is it to inform or to sell?
- if the text is selling something, use positive and enthusiastic language
- be consistent when you translate place names, such as Krak w / Cracow

The holiday rep game

6 You are a tour operator representative for a party of twenty tourists. Start at the airport, accompany your clients on holiday and follow all the instructions to get them safely home again.

GO!
HAVE A GOOD JOURNEY!

A tourist breaks his leg. Book him a flight home and go back one space.

It's started to rain. Plan an entertainment programme for the tourists.

The airline has lost your party's luggage. Ask for information from the airline.

One of your party has a problem with a restaurant bill. Complain to the waiter and go back two spaces.

Some of your party don't have swimming costumes. Suggest an alternative excursion.

You go to a restaurant. Describe a local dish to the tourists.

The tour bus has broken down. Apologise and go back to the start.

Sell an excursion or optional extra on the journey to the hotel.

The hotel has overbooked. Phone and book accommodation at another hotel.

Describe the new hotel and its facilities to your party.

Writing bank

Curriculum vitae (CV)

1 Use wide margins and leave lots of white space. It makes your CV easier to read.

2 Use a clear, easy-to-read typeface. Don't use *italics* or a small type size. Be consistent with the typefaces you use.

3 Make the section headings clear and leave a clear space between sections.

4 Separate each part of your work experience and education clearly.

5 Don't assume the reader will know what some abbreviations and acronyms mean. If in doubt, use the full name.

6 Don't exaggerate your talents but don't underestimate them either. Remember to sell yourself by using positive adjectives.

7 Watch out for grammar and spelling mistakes. Do a spell and grammar check on your computer when you finish your CV and ask someone else to check it for you.

Heading

Begin your CV with **personal details** including your name, address, telephone, email address and date of birth. Some people also include their place of birth, nationality and identity number. Your CV can also include an **objective,** describing the type of work you are hoping to do.

Body

The middle section of your CV gives details of your **work experience** and **education**. List your training, qualifications and work experience in reverse chronological order.
It's difficult to know what to write early in your career. If you don't have a lot of work experience, concentrate on your relevant free-time activities or unpaid experience.

Conclusion

End with other **relevant information** and your **references**. For example your special skills, free-time activities, any experience in voluntary organisations or participation in sports.
Offer references, although it is optional to give names and addresses. People often write *References available on request*.

Curriculum Vitae

Carla Hennessy

Personal details
131 Nelson Court, London W16, UK.
Telephone: +44 (0) 20 7946 0002
Email: clhennessy@mhp.uk
Date of birth: 13/3/1982
Place of birth: Hammersmith, London.

Nationality: British

Objective
To obtain a full-time position as waiter on a cruise liner that offers experience in a high standard of customer care.

Education and qualifications
1998: GNVQ Leisure and Tourism Diploma, Acton Tertiary College, London.
1996: 4 GCSEs – English, French, maths and biology, Acton Comprehensive School.

Employment history
1999 to present date: cocktail waiter, Magpie Hotel, Ealing, London.
1998: aerobics instructor, Acton Vale Youth Club, London.
1996 to 1998: shoe shop assistant (Saturdays only), Beta Shoes, Ealing, London.

Additional information
Active member of an amateur theatre group. Excellent computing skills.

References
Available on request.

Covering letter

1 In a personal letter you can put your name, address, telephone number and email on the right-hand or left-hand side of the letter.
2 There are different ways of writing dates: 15 April 2002, April 15th 2002, or 15/4/2002 but in US English the month comes first, e.g. 4/15/2002.
3 If you don't know the name of the person you are writing to, start with *Dear Sir / Madam*.
4 Write in short paragraphs so that the letter is well organised and easy to read.
5 When you don't know the name of the person you are writing to, close with *Yours faithfully*, followed by a comma.
6 Remember to write your full name clearly after your signature.

Charles Piper [1]
41, Sefton Road
Manchester
M19 8RU
chazpiper@hotmail.com

15th April, 2002 [2]

Dear Sir / Madam [3]

I am writing in reply to your advertisement in the *Manchester Evening Times* on Wednesday 12 April. I would like to apply for the position of Assistant Purser with Royal Mediterranean International.

I am an outgoing and motivated person and I also have strong communication and organisational skills. I have not worked on board a cruise ship before but I have experience as a hotel receptionist and I have the GNVQ Diploma in Leisure and Tourism. [4]

Please find enclosed a copy of my CV. I am available for interview at any time. I look forward to hearing from you.

Yours faithfully, [5]

Charles Piper

Charles Piper [6]

Formal letter

1 Use headed paper with the phone number, email address, etc. when writing on behalf of your hotel or company.

2 Remember to include the date. This is very important when filing correspondence.

3 You can include the address of the recipient on the left hand side of the letter.

4 You can include a reference number, code or title at the top of the letter.

5 When you know the name of the person, start with *Dear* and the correct title and name of the person followed by a comma.

6 Always make sure your letter is formal and polite. Use words like *please*, *thank you*, etc.

7 Organise your letter in short paragraphs.

8 When you know the name of the person, close with *Yours sincerely*.

9 Write your job position after your signature and name.

Sea View Hotel [1]
39 Beech Grove
Brighton BN2 3PD
Tel: 00 44 1265 8695925
Fax: 00 44 1265 8695926
email: seaview@brightonhotels.co.uk

20th November 2003 [2]

Dr Nicola Talbot
Flat A, 87 Monmouth Drive [3]
Oxford
OX5 2CG

Ref: guest questionnaire [4]

Dear Dr Nicola Talbot, [5]

Thank you for completing our questionnaire during your stay at our hotel last month.

We always appreciate hearing from our guests. Your comments are vital for us to continue improving our accommodation. We would like to apologise for the problems that you mentioned. The service you experienced is unusual and not the standard of our hotel. Please find enclosed a complimentary voucher for a night in one of our luxury hotels as compensation. [6]

Once again, we are sorry for any inconvenience caused during your stay and we hope that you will give us another chance to serve you. [7]

Yours sincerely, [8]

Andrew Millar

Andrew Millar
Hotel Manager [9]

Fax

1. Give a contact phone number if it is not on the letterhead.

2. Salutation – include the title (*Mrs, Miss, Ms, Mr, Dr,* and so on) and copy the name exactly as that person writes it. If you don't know the name or whether the person is a man or woman, put *Dear Sir or Madam.*

3. Reference line – this describes the main purpose of the fax or letter.

4. If you are responding to a letter, fax or email, refer to its subject and date in the first paragraph or sentence.

5. State the main reason for the fax in the first sentence. Remember that the recipient may have to read a lot of business correspondence.

6. The paragraphs of business letters and faxes can be short, usually between three and eight lines long. This helps the recipient to read and remember the important facts.

7. *Yours sincerely* is the most frequently-used closing expression. Only the first letter is capitalised.
   Kind regards, With best regards and *Best regards* are also possible for clients you know well as these are less formal.

8. Write your signature and type your name below the closing expression. Whenever possible, include your job title below your name.

Wilton Hotel

To	Mr Louis Fuller
Fax no.	(940) 284 3423
From	Miss Silvia Roth, Reservations Department, Wilton Hotel
Fax no.	(090) 784 1005
Phone no.	(090) 784 1003[1]
Date	November 26, 2009
Number of pages	1 of 1

Dear Mr Fuller,[2]

Confirmation of reservation[3]

In reply to your fax of today's date,[4] we are pleased to confirm your reservation.[5] I have included the information you will need to make your check-in as simple as possible.[6]

Your confirmation number: BF015H
Arrival date: January 10, 2010
Departure date: January 12, 2010
Room type: Double
Rate: $80.00
Your room will be ready for occupancy after 12 noon.

If any of this information is incorrect, please contact us immediately. If you have any additional questions, or need to make changes to this reservation, please fax us or call our phone number at the top of this fax. Thank you for choosing our hotel and I hope you enjoy your stay.

Yours sincerely,[7]

Silvia Roth

Silvia Roth

Reservations Manager[8]

Please note: Reservations cancelled without 24 hours' notice will be subject to a charge of one night's stay.

Email

1 Emails are often shorter and less formal than letters and faxes. However, it is perfectly acceptable to write very formal emails to people you do not know.
2 *cc* means a copy of this message was sent to this person.
3 Remember to check all times, dates and numbers before sending an email. It is easy to make a mistake.
4 *Regards*, or *Best regards*, can be used as the closing expression on a formal email.

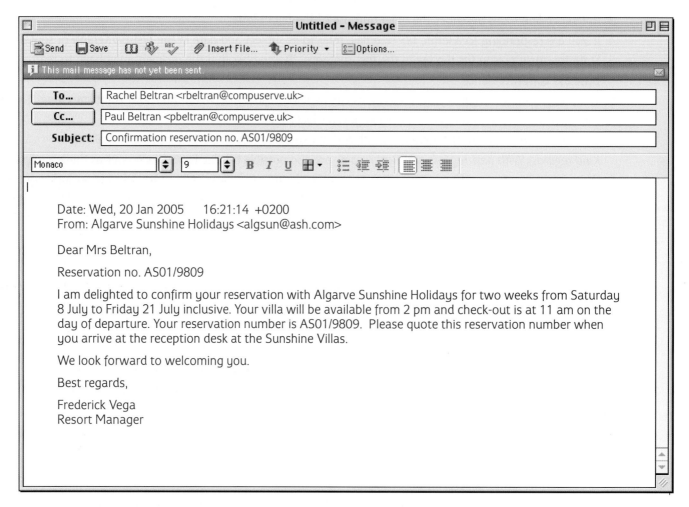

To... Rachel Beltran <rbeltran@compuserve.uk>
Cc... Paul Beltran <pbeltran@compuserve.uk>
Subject: Confirmation reservation no. AS01/9809

Date: Wed, 20 Jan 2005   16:21:14 +0200
From: Algarve Sunshine Holidays <algsun@ash.com>

Dear Mrs Beltran,

Reservation no. AS01/9809

I am delighted to confirm your reservation with Algarve Sunshine Holidays for two weeks from Saturday 8 July to Friday 21 July inclusive. Your villa will be available from 2 pm and check-out is at 11 am on the day of departure. Your reservation number is AS01/9809. Please quote this reservation number when you arrive at the reception desk at the Sunshine Villas.

We look forward to welcoming you.

Best regards,

Frederick Vega
Resort Manager

Other useful expressions

Making reference
With reference to your email of 7 February …
Thank you for your email of 7 February …

Explaining the reason for writing
I am writing to confirm / inform you that / apologise for / enquire about …

Apologising
I am sorry for any inconvenience caused by the delay on your recent flight …
I regret to tell you that we are fully booked for the dates …

Requesting
Please quote this reference number …
I would be grateful if you could confirm …

Offering
I am pleased to offer you …

Referring to future contact
I look forward to hearing from you.
We look forward to your stay at the … hotel in the future.
Please do not hesitate to contact us if you require any further information.

Referring to enclosed documents
I have enclosed / attached the timetable / your tickets / our brochure.

Pairwork files

Unit 1, Exercise 16

Student A

Answer your partner's questions about Anthony Grey. Then find out the same information about James Borras.

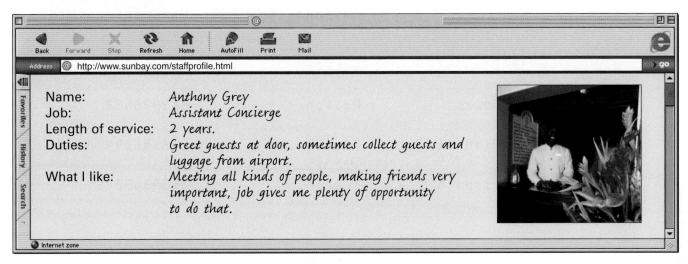

Name: *Anthony Grey*
Job: *Assistant Concierge*
Length of service: *2 years.*
Duties: *Greet guests at door, sometimes collect guests and luggage from airport.*
What I like: *Meeting all kinds of people, making friends very important, job gives me plenty of opportunity to do that.*

Name: *James Borras*
Job: ....
Length of service: *3 years.*
Duties: .... , ...
What I like: ....

Unit 2, Exercise 5

Student A

You are a travel agent. A customer phones about fly-drive deals to Tuscany. Recommend the Hotel Casa Giovane and answer the customer's questions.

Hotel Casa Giovane
San Gimignano

• 24 ROOMS • TWIN BEDROOMS HAVE SHOWERS • SATELLITE TV • PARKING
BED AND BUFFET BREAKFAST
MINIMUM STAY 3 NIGHTS
PISA: APPROX. 2 HOURS
FLORENCE: APPROX. 1 HOUR

Simply furnished and family run, this hotel has a highly-rated restaurant and represents excellent value for money. The quiet hotel gardens offer a small swimming pool and superb views across the Tuscan hills. Inside, the main lounge and bar have a cosy atmosphere. Casa Giovane is renowned for its excellent restaurant which serves local and national specialities.

PRICES BASED ON	BB	
TRANSFER TYPE INCLUDED	Car Hire	
No. OF NIGHTS	3	Extra Night
Apr 4 - May 1	375	42
May 2 - May 8	425	45
May 9 - May 29	415	44
May 30 - Jun 5	449	47
Jun 6 - Jul 3	435	45
Jul 4 - Jul 17	455	47
Jul 18 - Aug 18	515	48

DEPARTURE ON OR BETWEEN

Prices are per person sharing a twin room
Car hire is included from/to Pisa airport

Student A

Look at the information below and ask questions to complete the Sun Bay Hotel register.

What's the name of the guest in room 211?   Can you spell that for me?
Where's he/she from?   What's his/her passport number?

Room	Name	Nationality	Passport number
211	Mrs Andropov		
212	Mr Brandt	German	M582639001
308			
319	Ms Nowak	Polish	EG7435622
415			
417	Mr Bianchi	Italian	W75395144
502			
507	Mrs Dupont	French	J659863275

Student B

Look at the pictures of a mini-suite on the cruise ship *Arcadia*. Ask your partner questions to find out how it is different to the outside cabin that your partner has.

Is there a ... in your cabin?

MINI-SUITE

Two lower beds convertible to a king-size bed ● Bathroom with bath, shower and WC ● Walk-in wardrobe and drawer space ● Separate sitting area with sofa, chair and table ● Vanity table/writing desk ● TV, video and radio ● Safe, hairdryer and refrigerator ● Direct-dial telephone ● Floor-to-ceiling windows and patio door leading to balcony with chairs and table ● Fully air conditioned

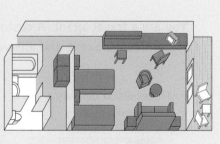

Unit 2, Exercise 15

Student B

You are travelling to Florida and want to book a hire car. Phone the car hire agent and make the following reservation.

> Chevrolet Lumina with air con.
> Pick up car at Miami airport on 12 Aug at 8.30 am.
> Drop off car at Miami airport on 26 Aug at 1 pm.
> Cost for 2 weeks?

Unit 5, Exercise 14

Student A

Look at the information about the Hotel Giorgione below and answer your partner's questions. Then ask your partner for information about the Hotel Europa e Regina. Write five sentences comparing the hotels.

Giorgione

Santi Apostoli, Cannaregio 4587.

☎ 041 522 58 10 FAX 041 523 90 92

@ giorgione@hotelgiorgione.com

Rooms: 68 🛏 1 ⊞ ↗ TV ▤
🍴 ≋ 🛄 €€€€

This is a modern, recently refurbished hotel in a delightful, colour-washed building. There is a spacious reception area and bar and a charming garden. It is conveniently situated in the Rialto area.

Student A

Look at the pictures of an outside twin cabin on the cruise ship *Arcadia*. Ask your partner questions to find out how it is different to the mini-suite that your partner has.

Does your cabin have ... ?

OUTSIDE TWIN CABIN

Two lower beds convertible to a king-size bed ● Bathroom with shower and WC ● Walk-in wardrobe and drawer space ● Easy chair, table and stool ● Vanity table / writing desk ● TV and radio ● Safe, hairdryer and refrigerator ● Direct-dial telephone ● Large picture window (porthole on F deck) ● Fully air conditioned

 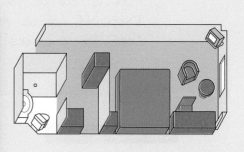

TWIN AS A SINGLE CABIN

Some of these cabins are available as single cabins.

Student A

You are going to apply for a job with Royal Mediterranean International. Give your covering note and CV to your partner who is going to interview you.

Before the interview

- read the advertisement again very carefully
- think about why you want the job and why you would be good at it
- make a list of your strengths and abilities
- make a list of questions the interviewer might ask you. How will you answer them?
- make a list of questions to ask the interviewer

During the interview

- shake the interviewer's hand and introduce yourself
  Pleased to meet you, I'm ...
- say why you would be good for the job
  I think I'd be good for the job because I have experience in ...
- be friendly and confident
- give positive answers and be enthusiastic
  I really enjoy working with people.
- ask questions, show interest and take notes
  What hours would I work?
  Would there be any training opportunities?

Unit 1, Exercise 16

Student B

Find out the following information about Anthony Grey from your partner. Then answer your partner's questions about James Borras.

Name: _Anthony Grey_ ....

Job: ....

Length of service: _2 years._

Duties: .... _at door, sometimes_ ....

What I like: ....

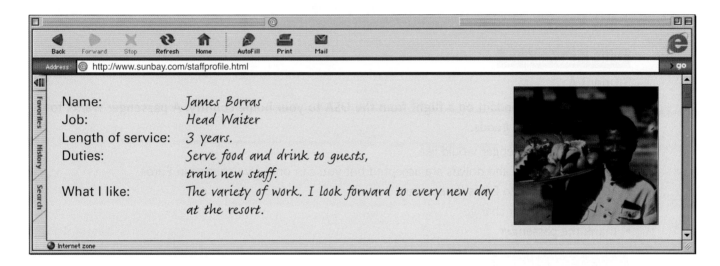

Name: _James Borras_
Job: _Head Waiter_
Length of service: _3 years._
Duties: _Serve food and drink to guests, train new staff._
What I like: _The variety of work. I look forward to every new day at the resort._

Address: http://www.sunbay.com/staffprofile.html

Unit 9, Exercise 5

Student A

Look at the security procedures on page 59 and prepare questions to ask passengers at check-in.

Is all your baggage securely closed and locked?
Do you have labels on all your baggage?

When you have prepared your questions, work with your partner to make a check-in dialogue.

Consolidation 1, Exercise 8

Student A

You are a receptionist at the Hotel Rialto. Deal with Peter or Amy Harrison. The hotel manager is at lunch. Listen and explain the points in the manager's note on page 39. You are not in a position to give them any compensation so try to offer another solution. Choose one or more of these possible solutions to the problem:

a) Explain that Mr and Mrs Harrison should contact Sunny Planet Holidays.

b) Offer them two free tickets to the opera.

c) Ask them to return when the manager is in the office.

d) Offer to upgrade their room to the suites that overlook the canal – at an additional charge of 40%.

e) Contact Sunny Planet Holidays yourself.

Unit 9, Exercise 7

Student B

You are a passenger on a plane flying economy class to London from New York. Ask the cabin crew about the following things:

- change to business class?
- where to put my hand luggage?
- smoke?
- use my mobile phone?
- use my laptop?
- fill out a landing card if not from the European Union?
- have a vegetarian meal?

Unit 9, Exercise 13

Student A

You are a flight attendant on a flight from the USA to your home country. A passenger wants to buy some duty-free goods.

- ask what the passenger would like
- explain that Euros and dollars are accepted but you can only give change in Euros
- convert the price to Euros if necessary
- give the passenger change
- thank the passenger

Unit 10, Exercise 12

Student A

You are a receptionist at a hotel in Cracow. Suggest some of these places to the guest.

LAZNIA

Open 18.00 until late
Alternative student pub
in a cellar with theatre,
bands, films.

West End

open 09.00 - 09.00

A café / pub dedicated
to film. Directors like
Spielberg and Tarantino
have their own director's
chairs. Films with subtitles
are shown regularly.

CELLAR PUBS

U Louisa open 11.00 – 24.00
Centrally located pub with blues music.
During the break you can surf
in the internet café.

Unit 11, Exercise 4

Student A

You are a tourist. Prepare some questions asking for information about some of the following:

- the local scenery in general
- any special 'star sights' that are worth visiting, e.g. volcanoes, fjords, etc.
- local wildlife – you are interested in animals
- national parks or mountains – you would like to do some walking
- beaches or lakes – you would like to go swimming or do some water sports

Unit 11, Exercise 15

Student A

You are a travel agent. A customer calls to confirm the following reservation. Check the following details and make the booking.

- ask for the booking reference number
- ask what changes the customer would like to make
- ask for payment details
- check and confirm the new details
- promise to confirm the changes in writing
- thank the customer for calling

Tour details	Reference: PT30574 / 22
Name of tour:	Adventure Paradise
Number of people:	4 adults
Number of days:	7, starting 15 March
Accommodation:	2 twin rooms
Excursions:	rafting, bungee jumping, mountain biking,
	flightseeing
Payment details:	
Method:	cheque
Card number:	
Expiry date:	

Consolidation 1, Exercise 8

Student B

You are Peter / Amy Harrison. You are dissatisfied with the Hotel Rialto. Ask to see the hotel manager. You think the hotel is substandard and Venice is expensive. Explain the points mentioned in your letter on page 38. Ask to move rooms. You are not prepared to pay any extra.

Student A

You are at the reception desk at the ski lodge below. Ask for directions to these places. Then use the expressions on page 81 to give your partner directions from reception.

swimming pool   baby changing facilities   ski-hire office   bar

Lounge

Reception

Main entrance

Car park

Locker room

Resort rep's office

Swimming pool

Dining room

Consolidation 3, Exercise 4

Student A

Write sentences to describe the following items.

hairdryer   receptionist   porter   towel   menu   knife
credit card   concierge   coach   backpack   tour guide

It's something that you use to dry your hair.
It's someone who answers the phone at a hotel.

Unit 13, Exercise 18

Student A

Ask your partner for health and safety information for travelling to Thailand. Ask about:

- personal safety when travelling / staying in hotels
- availability of medicines
- common health problems for travellers
- any necessary precautions

Now look at the safety advice for travellers to South Africa and answer your partner's questions.

Travelling in South Africa

Although many inner cities and townships can be dangerous, especially at night, South Africa is generally safe for travellers who take reasonable precautions. Never go out on your own. Don't wear expensive clothes or carry large amounts of money with you. Use the hotel safe-deposit box. Pickpockets are a problem, as are muggers, who snatch handbags and run away. When driving always keep the doors locked and don't stop to give people a lift. Tap water is generally safe to drink and travellers to South Africa usually don't suffer from stomach upsets. On safari, animals should always be respected and there are some poisonous spiders and snakes. Always carry a small medical pack when on safari. Malaria and bilharzia occur in certain areas.

Unit 14, Exercise 6

Student B

You are checking out of the Admiral Hotel. You think there is a mistake with the bill below. Ask the receptionist about the car park charge and the check-out charge. Explain that you have not got a car.

The Admiral Hotel

02/765
Room number 233

Bed and buffet breakfast 2 nights @ 2650	5300
Car park fee	180
Minibar	34
Registration fee	87
Check-out	56
Tax (7%)	396
Total	RUR 6053

Unit 14, Exercise 11

Student A

You are a receptionist at the Admiral Hotel in St Petersburg. Deal with the hotel guests at registration.

- Offer to upgrade the guest's room.
- Offer the business traveller a mini-suite which has space for meetings or a meetings room in the conference centre.
- Welcome the guest. They have stayed at the Admiral Hotel in the past. Today they look especially tired. Offer to upgrade their room.

Unit 14, Exercise 16

Student A

You are a business traveller checking out of a four-star hotel in your city or area.

- Ask for the bill. Check that the bill is correct.
- Listen to the information the front-desk clerk tells you. Decide whether or not you want to re-book. If you book a better room, you will have to justify the extra cost to your company.
- Ask the receptionist to send any useful information to your secretary.

Consolidation 3, Exercise 4

Student B

Write sentences to describe the following items.

| telephone   chambermaid   chef   key   glass   suitcase   safe   travel agent   plane   passport |

It's something that you use to speak to people who are a long way away.
It's someone who cleans hotel rooms.

Unit 14, Exercise 6

Student A

You are a receptionist at the Admiral Hotel. Explain to the guest that your hotel charges extra for use of the car park and for guests checking out before 7 am.

Unit 11, Exercise 15

Student B

You reserved a seven-day tour of Queenstown, New Zealand. Call the travel agent, confirm the booking and make the following changes to the booking. Your booking reference was PT30574 / 22.

- there are now five adults in the group, not four
- the time spent in Queenstown will be six days, not seven, starting on 15 March
- you had reserved excursions for rafting, bungee jumping, mountain biking and flightseeing. Change one of these activities
- you want to pay by Visa card

Unit 10, Exercise 12

Student B

You are a tourist in Cracow. You would like to go out this evening but you also want to go home early because tomorrow your coach tour leaves at 7 am. Ask the receptionist to recommend some places. You are interested in these activities:

    the internet   films   theatre / cabaret   cafés   eating ice cream

Unit 11, Exercise 4

Student B

You work in your local tourist office. Give Student A some information about your country's scenery and any 'star sights' in the area. Make notes of the sights you will recommend and why they are 'star sights'.

Student B

You are checking in at the Admiral Hotel in St Petersburg.

- You are a first-time guest. You are unhappy with your room and would like a better room. You don't mind paying a little extra.
- You are a business traveller. Your secretary booked a standard room. Your business plans have changed and now you need to have meetings at the hotel.
- You are a repeat guest. You booked a standard room last time you stayed, but today you have had a very long journey.

Unit 11, Exercise 11

Student A

WORLD BREAKS

Activities	Duration (days)	Price	Departure times
White water rafting			
Nevis Whitewater	1	$119 – $170	....................................[1]
Kawarau River rafting	1	$199	9.00 am
Bungee jumping			
Kawarau Bridge	2 hours	...................[2]	by individual arrangement
.......................[3]	2 hours	$119	by individual arrangement
Mountain biking			
....................[4]	..............[5]	...............[6]	–
Lake Wanaka	2	From $45	–
Flightseeing			
Lake Wakatipu Tours	1	$339	..................................[7]
Remarkable Mountains	1	...............[8]	9.15 am & 12.45 pm

Valid 1 October 2002 – 30 September 2003
Note: Prices subject to change

Grammar reference

Adverbs of frequency

1 Adverbs of frequency go after the verb *be*.

*The hotel is **usually** busy in October.*

2 With other verb forms, adverbs of frequency go before the main verb.

*Our customers **never** complain.*
*It can **sometimes** be difficult to find a taxi at night.*
*They have **often** been to Turkey.*

Present simple

1 We use *don't* or *doesn't* to form negatives.

*We **don't clean** the windows every day.*
*Darina **doesn't go** to work on Tuesdays.*

2 We use *do* or *does* to form questions.

***Do** you **clean** the mirrors? **Does** Darina **go** to work on Sundays?*

3 Short form answers.

Do you use a computer? Yes, I do. / No, I don't.
Does she like her job? Yes, she does. / No, she doesn't.

Spelling

1 We usually add *-s* to the verb to make the *he / she / it* form of the present simple.

clean / cleans, check / checks, make / makes

2 If the verb ends in a consonant + *y*, the *y* changes to *i* and we add *-es*.

tidy / tidies, carry / carries, fly / flies.

Use

3 We use the present simple to talk about routines, habits, actions and situations that happen all the time.

*I **help** the Head Housekeeper.*
*A stay-over **is** a general routine clean.*

Typical mistakes

- We do not use the present simple to express offers or suggestions.

I help you? = Can I help you?

- We do not use the present simple to express future actions.

I check for you = I'll check for you.

- We do not use the present simple to talk about temporary situations or actions.

I work in London this summer = I'm working in London this summer.

Present continuous

We use *be* + verb + *-ing* to form the present continuous.

*We're **staying** in Miami for a few days.*
*You **aren't spending** any time in Orlando.*
*When **are** you **arriving** in Florida?*

Short answers

Are you going to Florida? Yes, I am. / No, I'm not.
Is he flying to Florida? Yes, he is. / No, he isn't. / No, he's not.

Spelling

1 If the verb ends in *-e*, we do not include the final *e* before *-ing*:

close / closing, take / taking, come / coming, give / giving

2 If the verb ends in *-y*, add *-ing* and the spelling does not change:

study / studying, carry / carrying, enjoy / enjoying

3 *Be* and *see* are different.

be / being, see / seeing

4 In UK English, verbs that end in *-l* change to *-ll* in the *-ing* or *-ed* form.

travel / travelling / travelled, cancel / cancelling / cancelled

5 We also double the final consonant of these verbs before *-ing* or *-ed*.

stop / stopped / stopping, plan / planning / planned, rob / robbing / robbed

If the verb has more than one syllable, we only double the final consonant if the final syllable is stressed.

begin / beginning, prefer / preferring / preferred

Use

1 We use the present continuous to describe activities that are happening now.

*Jane **is talking** to the travel agent at the moment.*

2 We use the present continuous to describe temporary activities.

*We **are studying** tourism this year.*

3 Some verbs are not used in the continuous form.

Janet is being a travel agent. = Janet is a travel agent.
Oscar isn't having time to meet Jackie. = Oscar doesn't have time to meet Jackie.

4 We also use the present continuous for planned future arrangements.

*Jane **is travelling** to Florida on 17 May.*
*Oscar **isn't meeting** Jackie.*

Unit 3

Countable and uncountable nouns

1 Countable nouns are things we can count.

hotels, rooms, guests, dollars

2 Uncountable nouns are things we can't count.

tourism, weather, water

3 We use *a/an* with single countable nouns, e.g. *a beach*. We cannot usually use *a/an* with uncountable nouns.

~~*a sand*~~ *= some sand*

4 We use *some* and *any* with plural countable nouns and uncountable nouns. *Some* is used in positive sentences and *any* is used in negative sentences and questions.

*There are **some** beautiful beaches near here.*
*There is **some** sand on my towel.*
*There aren't **any** towels in the room.*
*Is there **any** room service after 10 pm?*

5 We use *many* and *a lot (of)* with plural countable nouns.

many tourists, a lot of tourists

6 We use *much* and *a lot (of)* with uncountable nouns.

much food, a lot of food

7 *Many* and *much* are more common in questions and negatives. We usually use *a lot (of)* in positive sentences.

*Did you take **many** photographs?*
*She didn't drink **much** water.*
*There were **a lot of** people on the beach.*

8 Many nouns can be used as countable and uncountable nouns, usually with a difference in meaning.

She ordered chicken. (A portion or dish.)
She ordered a chicken. (A whole chicken.)

9 Drinks are usually uncountable. But they can be countable if it's a cup or a glass.

We'd like two teas and a coffee.
An orange juice and a tonic water, please.

Typical mistakes

• Some nouns which are uncountable in English may be countable in other languages.

~~*I'd like an advice*~~ *= I'd like some advice.*
~~*He had a good travel*~~ *= He had a good journey/trip.*
~~*I need an information*~~ *= I need some information.*

• Other examples

furniture, news, money, weather, work

Unit 4

Past simple

1 We add *-ed* to regular past simple verbs to form the past. Irregular verbs have their own forms as listed on page 131.

*I **watched** the Olympics on television.*
*We **saw** the Sagrada Familia yesterday.*

2 We use *did* to form negatives and questions.

*We **didn't see** the fountain.*
*What **did** she **say**?*

Short answers

Did you book a holiday last week? Yes, I did. / No, I didn't.
Did she book a holiday last week? Yes, she did. / No, she didn't.

Typical mistakes

We ~~go~~ walking in Zakopane last summer.
We went walking in Zakopane last summer.

I ~~didn't stayed~~ in a four star hotel.
I didn't stay in a four star hotel.

How long ~~stayed you~~ in Venice?
How long did you stay in Venice?

~~*You liked*~~ *the tour?*
Did you like the tour?

~~*You was*~~ *in Germany last week?*
Were you in Germany last week?

They ~~don't win~~ the football match against Barcelona.
They didn't win the football match against Barcelona.

Use

1 We use the past simple to talk about finished actions at a definite time in the past.

*When **did the coach leave**?*
*They **didn't return** to the hotel until 6.00 pm.*

2 The past simple is often used with these time expressions.

***Did** you **watch** TV yesterday / yesterday evening?*
*He **sent** the email last night / Tuesday / week / month / year.*
*We **didn't have** many customers six hours / months / years ago.*
*When **did** visitors **start** coming to the island?*

Unit 5

Comparative and superlative adjectives

1 We form comparatives and superlatives of one-syllable adjectives, or those that end in -y, as follows.

One-syllable adjectives and two-syllable adjectives ending in -y			
high cheap safe	high**er** (than) cheap**er** (than) saf**er** (than)	**the** high**est** **the** cheap**est** **the** saf**est**	Most one-syllable adjectives form the comparative and superlative with -er and -est.
large	larg**er** (than)	**the** larg**est**	One-syllable adjectives ending in -e form the comparative and superlative with -r and -st.
big	big**ger** (than)	**the** big**gest**	One-syllable adjectives ending in a vowel and a consonant form the comparative and superlative with a double consonant.
tidy early	tid**ier** (than) earl**ier** (than)	**the** tid**iest** **the** earl**iest**	Two-syllable adjectives that end with -y form the comparative and superlative with -ier and -iest.

2 We make the comparative and superlative with *more* and *the most* for:

• Most adjectives with two or more syllables.

modern / **more** modern / **the most** modern
comfortable / **more** comfortable / **the most** comfortable

3 Adjectives with one syllable that end in -ed.

organised / **more** organised / **the most** organised

4 We can use *much* or *far* to modify a comparative.

New York is **much bigger** than London.
This room is **far more comfortable** than the other one.

5 We use *(not) as … as* and the simple adjective in comparisons of equality.

Is Amsterdam **as** big **as** London?
The hotel was**n't as** good **as** we expected.

6 Irregular forms

good / better / the best
bad / worse / the worst
far / further / the furthest

Unit 6

Present perfect

The past participle of regular verbs ends in -ed. For a list of irregular verbs see page 131.

*The dancing competition **has started** on the prom deck.*
***Have** you **taken** your sea-sickness pills?*

Short answers

Have you ever been to India? Yes, I have. / No, I haven't.
Has she ever flown before? Yes, she has. / No, she hasn't.

Use

We use the present perfect to describe:

1 A life experience

*We **have worked** as tour guides. (at some time in our lives)*
***Have you ever been** to Mexico? (at some time in your life)*

2 An event that hasn't happened yet:

*I **have never been** to Brazil.*
*I **haven't been** to Brazil yet. (I'm going in the near future)*

3 A recent event:

*I've **already checked** their passports.*
*The plane's **already left.***

4 To describe an event that started in the past and is continuing in the present. We often use the time expressions *for* or *since* with the present perfect.

*I have lived in Barcelona **for** 12 years. (I still live in Barcelona.)*
*He has worked as a tour guide **since** 1999. (He's working as a tour guide now.)*

We use *for* with periods of time and *since* for points in time, when something began.

Typical mistakes
~~Did you ever worked~~ abroad? Have you ever worked abroad?
Have you ever been ~~in~~ Ireland? Have you ever been to Ireland?
I ~~don't see~~ you since last Friday. I haven't seen you since last Friday.
When ~~have you started~~ the course? When did you start the course?

Polite requests and offers

1 We use the modal verb *could* in polite requests.

Could you repeat that, please?
Could I see your passport, please?

2 *Would / Do you mind* + verb + *-ing*? also expresses a polite request.

Would you mind closing the door?
Do you mind not smoking in this area?

3 *Would you like ...?* is used to make a polite offer.

Would you like to see the wine list?
Would you like me to call a taxi?

Giving advice and recommendations

1 We use the modal verb *should* for giving recommendations and advice.

You **should** drink lots of water.
You **shouldn't** carry a lot of cash.

Typical mistakes

• We use the infinitive without *to* after a modal verb.
You should to carry some identification.
You should carry some identification.

2 Other structures for giving advice and recommendations.

It's best + to + infinitive
It's a good idea + to + infinitive
I recommend you + verb
Avoid + verb + -ing

It's best to visit the region in May or June.
I recommend you visit the Prado museum.
Avoid wearing a lot of jewellery.

3 We can use the modal verb *must* for giving strong recommendations.

You **must** try our national dish.
You **mustn't** walk around the town centre late at night.

Going to + verb

1 We use *going to* for predictions with evidence in the present.

*There's a lot of traffic. It's **going to be** faster to take the metro.*

2 We use *going to* for future intentions when we have decided to do something before the moment speaking.

*The tourist board is **going to build** more hotels next year.*

Short answers
Is it going to rain tomorrow? Yes, it is. / No, it isn't.
Are you going to stay another night, sir? Yes I am. / No, I'm not.

Will + infinitive

1 We use *will / won't* for predictions with or without present evidence.

*We think the new hotel **will be** very popular. (In our opinion.)*
*Local people probably **won't want** a new airport.*

2 We use *will / won't* for decisions made at the time of speaking.

*I'**ll phone** you tomorrow.*

Typical mistakes

I don't will have time to phone you tomorrow.
I won't have time to phone you tomorrow.

They probably will build a bar on the beach.
They will probably build a bar on the beach.

They won't probably leave until the afternoon.
They probably won't leave until the afternoon.

may / might + infinitive

When we talk about future possibilities, we can use *may* or *might*.

*They **may / might build** more roads in the future.*

Typical mistakes

There don't might be enough rooms.
There might not / mightn't be enough rooms.

Unit 9

Modal verbs (obligation)

1 We use the modal verbs *must* and *have to* (see below) when something is absolutely necessary.

*Passengers **must wear** their seatbelts during take-off and landing.*
*She **had to switch off** her mobile phone during the flight.*

2 We use *mustn't* and *can't* when something is not permitted.

*Passengers **mustn't smoke** in the toilets on board.*

3 We use *should* for giving recommendations and advice. (See Unit 7)

*Passengers **should contact** United Airlines for further details.*

4 We use *can* and *may* to express permission.

*You **can smoke** in the designated areas.*

Typical mistakes

- We use the infinitive without *to* after a modal verb.
You must ~~to check in~~ ninety minutes before the flight.
You must check in ninety minutes before the flight.

Have to

1 We use the modal verb *have to* when something is absolutely necessary. We use it similarly to *must*.
*You **have to check in** ninety minutes before the flight.*

2 We use *don't/doesn't have to* when something is not necessary.

*She has one small bag so she **doesn't have to check in** any luggage.*

Short answers
Do we have to check in now? Yes, you do./No, you don't.
Does she have to go? Yes, she does./No, she doesn't.

Typical mistakes

- Have to needs the auxiliary *do/does* to form the negative and question forms.
~~He hasn't to return~~ to Moscow until August.
He doesn't have to return to Moscow until August.
~~Have we to~~ wait long?
Do we have to wait long?

Unit 10

Modal verbs (*can, could, might*)

1 We use *can* for possible options or simple facts.
*You **can get** a train or coach to Warsaw from Cracow.*
*We **can divide** the conference room into three sections.*

2 We use *can/could* for recommending things or making suggestions.
*You **can/could see** a lot of art galleries in Cracow.*
***Can/could** we **go** dancing this evening?*

3 We also use *can/could* for making offers and requests. (See Unit 7)

4 We also use the model verb *might* for recommending, especially before the verbs *like* or *want*.
*You **might like/want to go** early because there are always long queues.*

Typical mistakes

- We use the infinitive without *to* after a modal verb.
~~Can we to~~ go to the cinema this weekend?
Can we go to the cinema this weekend?
We ~~could to~~ sit outside a café for dinner.
We could sit outside a café for dinner.

- We also use *might* for future possibilities. (See Unit 8)

Unit 11

Future forms

Present simple (See Unit 1)

1 We use the present simple for timetables, programmes and schedules.

*The coach **leaves** at 10 pm.*
*Our plane **doesn't land** until 5.40 in the morning.*

Present continuous (See Unit 2)

2 We use the present continuous for future plans and personal arrangements.

*We**'re** probably **spending** Easter in Turkey.*
*What **are** you **doing** for your summer holidays?*

Typical mistakes

- We don't use the present simple to talk about future plans and arrangements.
~~I go to~~ work early tomorrow.
I'm going to work early tomorrow.

Present passive

We form the present passive with *be* + past participle.

*The hotel **is located** in the centre of the village.*
*Children must **be accompanied** by an adult.*

Short answers

Are the chair lifts checked daily? Yes, they are. / No, they aren't.
Is the ski instructor contracted by the tour operator? Yes, she is. / No, she isn't.

Past passive

We form the past passive with *was / were* + past participle.

***Was** the room **reserved**?*
*Most of the rooms **were booked** some time ago.*

Short answers

Was the manager trained in Switzerland? Yes, he was. / No, he wasn't.
Were the winter Olympic Games held in Salt Lake City? Yes, they were. / No, they weren't.

Use

1 We often use the passive for describing processes.

*Most ski resort hotels **are occupied** at the weekends.*

2 We use *by* to show the person or thing that does the action.

*The rooms **were booked by** the company secretary.*

3 When we do not know who was responsible, or if it is not important, we do not use *by*.

*The students **are taught** English and French (by teachers).*
*The hotel **was redecorated** (by a painter) last year.*

Typical mistakes

The trainees ~~were place~~ with international hotels.
The trainees were placed with international hotels.

English ~~is speaking~~ here.
English is spoken here.

Giving instructions

We use the imperative to give instructions.

***Go** downstairs, turn right and you'll see the ski hire office.*
***Be** careful not to hit other skiers.*

Typical mistakes

• We don't use the imperative with a subject pronoun.
~~You turn left~~ and then right.
Turn left and then right.

• We use the auxiliary verb *don't* with the imperative.
~~Not drop~~ your ski poles.
Don't drop your ski poles.

Relative pronouns

1 *That*, *who* and *which* are relative pronouns. They join two sentences or two parts of a sentence. In defining relative clauses they give us essential information.

• We use *that* and *who* for people.
*The woman **who / that** spoke to you is the hotel manager.*

• We use *that* and *which* for things.
*This is the hotel **that / which** has a fantastic rooftop restaurant.*

Typical mistakes

• We don't use *he / she / it / they* with a relative pronoun.
The concierge ~~that he~~ works in the mornings reserved our theatre tickets.
The concierge that works in the mornings reserved our theatre tickets.

2 We use the pronouns *which* or *who* to give extra information about someone or something. These are called non-defining clauses. We use commas with these relative clauses.

The receptionist, who was very helpful, gave us our key.
The hotel, which opened in 2001, has a good reputation.

Conditionals

1 We use the zero conditional (*if* + present + present) for things that are always true. We can substitute *if* for *when*.

***When / if** a hotel **doesn't sell** its rooms, it **loses** money.*
*We **offer** a discount **if** you **book** in advance.*

2 We use the first conditional (*if* + present + modal verb + infinitive) for predicting results of future actions. We can substitute *will*, *might*, *can* or *going to*.

*If the receptionist **upsells** the guest **will** / **might re-book**.*
*We're **going to lower** our rates **if** we **don't get** more bookings.*

Short answers

Does a hotel lose money when it doesn't sell its rooms? Yes, it does. / No, it doesn't.
Will I get a commission if I sell more rooms? Yes, you will. / No, you won't.

Typical mistakes

- We only use a comma after the *if*-clause when it comes at the beginning of the sentence.

If you like I'll send you our brochure.
If you like, I'll send you our brochure. But, I'll send you our brochure if you like.

- We do not use *will* in the *if*-clause.

If travellers will be tired, they upgrade their room.
If travellers are tired, they will upgrade their room.

Verb lists

Stative verbs

There are several verbs that are not generally used in the continuous form. These are called stative verbs. The most common ones are:

1 Verbs expressing likes and dislikes

dislike, hate, like, love, need, prefer, want, wish
*We **want** a room with a sea view.*

2 Verbs expressing opinions and beliefs

believe, doubt, feel, imagine, know, recognise, see, suppose, think, understand
*I **think** Costa Rica would be a great place to visit.*

3 Verbs expressing the properties something or someone has

appear, be, contain, cost, have, include, lack, look, measure, seem, smell, sound, taste, weigh
*This fish **tastes** strange but it **smells** fine.*

4 Verbs related to possession

belong to, have, own, need
*This hotel **belongs to** a chain.*

Irregular verbs

These verbs are irregular in the past simple.

be	was / were	been
become	became	become
begin	began	begun
break	broke	broken
bring	brought	brought
build	built	built
buy	bought	bought
choose	chose	chosen
come	came	come
cost	cost	cost
cut	cut	cut
do	did	done
drink	drank	drunk
drive	drove	driven
eat	ate	eaten
fall	fell	fallen
feel	felt	felt
find	found	found
fly	flew	flown
forget	forgot	forgotten
get	got	got
give	gave	given
go	went	gone
have	had	had
hear	heard	heard
hit	hit	hit
hold	held	held
keep	kept	kept
know	knew	known
leave	left	left
let	let	let
lose	lost	lost
make	made	made
meet	met	met
pay	paid	paid
put	put	put
read	read	read
ring	rang	rung
say	said	said
see	saw	seen
sell	sold	sold
send	sent	sent
sit	sat	sat
speak	spoke	spoken
spend	spent	spent
swim	swam	swum
take	took	taken
tell	told	told
think	thought	thought
understand	understood	understood
write	wrote	written

Tapescripts

Unit 1, Exercise 7 (CD Track 2)

I So, what do you do at the beginning of the day, Darina?

D I usually go to reception and meet the head housekeeper. There's usually a printout from the computer telling us which rooms are 'stay-overs' and which ones are 'check-outs'. We call the rooms 'SOs' and 'COs'.

I SOs and COs?

D That's right. An SO, or stay-over, is a general routine clean. We change the sheets every two days, towels every day if necessary, and clean the bathrooms.

I And what about the bedrooms?

D In the bedroom we make the bed, clean and tidy up. If people are staying over, we just give it a quick tidy and don't disturb their things.

Unit 1, Exercise 9 (CD Track 3)

I So, how many days a week do you work?

D Six days a week.

I And do you have to work on Saturdays and Sundays?

D I always work on Saturdays and Sundays.

I So do you have any free days?

D I always take Tuesdays or Wednesdays.

I And what time do you finish work at the hotel?

D I often work from nine to one, or nine to two, but on a very busy day, especially if it's a Monday with a lot of check-outs, sometimes I don't finish until three in the afternoon.

Unit 1, Exercise 11 (CD Track 4)

I What are you responsible for as Assistant Housekeeper?

D Well, I help the head housekeeper. We're responsible for about six people, six chambermaids, but sometimes eight in the summer with full occupancy. One of my main duties is to train new staff. Usually, on their first day, they stay with me all day. Then on the second day, they work with one of the chambermaids. I also have a bleeper so that people can contact me in case they have problems or any questions. When people have cleaned their rooms, I check everything's OK before the new guests check in.

Unit 2, Exercise 2 (CD Track 5)

TA Good afternoon, World Breaks, Janet Cookson speaking. How can I help you?

C Hello, I saw your advert in the newspaper for fly-drive holidays in Florida. Does that mean you get flights,

accommodation and car hire all included in the price?

TA That's right, madam.

C And what kind of accommodation is it?

TA Well, there are two options. You can have a self-catering apartment or stay in a hotel.

C We'd prefer an apartment, I think. How much will it cost for two weeks?

TA That all depends on when you travel. When are you thinking of going, madam?

C Well, some time when it's quieter, the second half of May. Is it off-season then?

TA Yes, it is. That's a very good time to go. We have a great offer at the moment: fourteen nights fly-drive with self-catering apartments for £543 per person.

C That sounds good. Could I book it now?

TA Certainly. Let me see, the flights are from London Heathrow on Thursdays, so that's Thursday 17th May, returning from Orlando, Florida on the morning of Thursday 31st May. How does that sound?

C That's fine.

TA Could I have the names of the people travelling, please?

C There's me, Jane Wright, my husband Simon and our son Andrew.

TA Could you spell your surname for me Mrs Wright?

C Yes, that's W-R-I-G-H-T.

TA OK, thank you. Just let me confirm the details. That's three people, two adults and one child, leaving London Heathrow on Thursday 17th May, returning on Thursday 31st May.

C Yes, that's right.

TA Thank you, Mrs Wright. Now how do you wish to pay for your holiday? By credit card?

Unit 2, Exercise 8 (CD Track 6)

J Hello.

O Jackie. It's Oscar. How are you?

J Oh, hi, Oscar.

O Did I wake you up?

J No, but I'm going to bed soon. It's late here.

O Yeah, sorry. Listen, do you want to meet then, when I'm in Florida?

J Yeah, sure. When did you say you're arriving? The 15th?

O Yeah, that's right. Orlando airport.

J And how are you getting around Florida?

O I'm hiring a car at the airport.

J And I suppose you're driving straight to Disney World.

O Of course, and Universal Studios. Do you want to come?

J No, I can't. I'm working that week. But why don't we meet at Daytona Beach at the weekend? It's not that far from Orlando.

O Maybe, but I really want to see the Kennedy Space Center. And then at the weekend I'm meeting John Hamilton. Do you remember him from college?

J Yeah, I remember John.

O We're going scuba-diving and then we're driving through the Everglades National Park. I'm really looking forward to it.

J So, you aren't spending any time in Orlando at all.

O Not really. You see, we're staying in Miami for a few days. John knows some friends there. And we're driving straight up to the Panhandle after that. You know, we want to spend some time relaxing on the beach. See Florida's best beaches and all that.

J Right, so maybe when you're not doing anything special one day, you can phone me.

O What? Jackie? Jackie? What did I say?

Unit 2, Exercise 13 (CD Track 7)

A Hello, Miami Autos Direct. How can I help you?

C Hello, I'd like to hire a car. I called yesterday.

A Can I have your name, please, sir?

C It's Craig. Mr Philip Craig.

A Just one moment, sir. Was that a Group B car?

C That's right. The Chevrolet Monte Carlo with air conditioning.

A And you'd like seven-day rental from Miami International Airport. Are you returning to Miami Airport?

C Yes, we are. Could you confirm the price? You said it was $470 including insurance.

A Uhuh. Plus tax at 6.5%.

C Sorry, could you repeat that please?

A You also have to pay 6.5% tax.

C Oh. Oh, I didn't know that.

A Are you and your family US nationals?

C No, we're British.

A Well. For non-US nationals we strongly recommend you take out additional liability insurance.

C Additional insurance?

A That's right, sir. ALI gives additional third-party liability in case of accidents and injury.

C Oh. Well, I suppose we should take that too.

A And when are you picking up the car, Mr Craig?

C Tomorrow morning at 9 am.

A Great, see you at nine and thanks for calling! Have a nice day.

C Hang on! So, what's the total cost?

Unit 2, Exercise 14 (CD Track 8)

1 How can I help you?

2 Can I have your name, please, sir?

3 Just one moment, sir.

4 Sorry, could you repeat that, please?

5 Thank you for calling!

Unit 3, Exercise 10 (CD Track 9)

Group 1

rice, juice, milk, salt, prawn, fruit, meal, food

Group 2

chocolate, omelette, coffee, salmon, sugar, chicken, sandwich, lettuce, pizza, salad, curry

Group 3

broccoli, vegetable, aubergine,

Group 4

potato, spaghetti, tomato

Unit 3, Exercise 16 (CD Track 10)

One

C Excuse me!

W I'll be with you in a minute, sir. Is everything all right, sir?

C Well, actually, I think you overcharged us for the water.

W Let me see. It says two bottles of sparkling water.

C But we only had one bottle.

W I'm sorry. I'm afraid there's been a mistake. I'll ask the cashier to deduct one bottle.

C Thank you.

Two

W You know this group booking for twelve people?

M Yes, they're actors from the theatre. They're usually late but they're regular customers.

W Well, four of them haven't arrived yet and the others are getting impatient.

M Have you taken their drinks orders yet?

W Er, no, not yet.

M Well, hurry up and if the others don't arrive in fifteen minutes, take the orders from the diners that are here!

W Yes, of course, sir.

W Good evening, are you ready to order?

C Oh, at last. We've been waiting for hours!

W I'm very sorry, sir. I'm afraid we're very busy this evening.

Three

C Excuse me, but this steak is too rare.

W I'm sorry, sir.

C I'd like it medium, please.

W   Certainly, I'll ask the chef to put it back under the grill, sir. Here you are. One medium steak.
C   But this one's burnt!
W   Er, I thought you said medium, sir.
C   I can't eat that! It's overdone!
W   Ah, then I'll bring another one right away.

Unit 4, Exercise 12 (CD Track 11)

J   And on your left you can see the sculpture, *Woman and Bird* by the famous Catalan artist, Joan Miró ...
T1   It doesn't look like a woman to me, dad.
T2   Sssh!
J   Now our next stop in Barcelona is the famous *Magic Fountains* in Plaça d'Espanya. The fountains were built in er, um, ... quite a long time ago. This show of beautiful coloured fountains first started at the time of the Olympic Games, in 1992. Maybe you saw them on television. Do you remember the song *Barcelona* by Freddie Mercury and the well-known opera singer, Montserrat Caballé? And now you can see the Magic Fountains most evenings in the summer. There's a show every half hour.
T3   What time does the next show start?
J   Let me see. There's one starting in five minutes, at 9.30.
T3   And how long does it take?
J   About half an hour. Please be back at the bus by 10.15.
T4   Excuse me, did you say the Olympic stadium was near here?
J   That's right, the sports stadium we visited this afternoon is further up the hill. This area is known as Montjuïc. You can see the fountains now straight ahead. Please be careful of pickpockets and look after your money and valuables.
T3   Excuse me, what did she say?
T2   Pickpockets – people who steal your money. So look after your bag.
T3   Oh, I see. Thank you. And how much does it cost to see the fountains?
J   Nothing, it's free.
T1   Hey, Dad, can we swim in the fountains?
T2   No, you can't swim in the fountains.
J   Here we are. No swimming is allowed in the fountains but if you'd like some refreshments or a drink, there's a café over there. This is the last stop on our tour today, so please be ready by a quarter past ten so we can be back at the hotel on time. Thank you.

Unit 5, Exercise 2 (CD Track 12)

One

I need a place where I can meet my clients because I don't want to go too far from the hotel. I need a stylish hotel with a first-class restaurant and first-class facilities. Swimming pool? No, I don't have time when I'm on business.

Two

Could I have a quiet room in a small or medium-sized hotel? I don't want to stay at the Piazza San Marco but it should be central. I'd like a place that's relaxing with friendly staff and maybe a courtyard or garden.

Unit 5, Exercise 9 (CD Track 13)

I   What made you decide to upgrade your hotel, Renee?
R   Well, for two reasons really. You see there is a lot of competition between hotels in Amsterdam, so your hotel has to be good. Secondly, I've noticed that tourists and businesspeople want a higher standard of accommodation than in the past.
I   So, how did you go about changing the hotel? What did you have to do?
R   Well, for one thing we had to make changes to the guestrooms. The rooms are now a lot more comfortable. The furniture's better quality and we've completely redecorated all the rooms in a more modern style. We also put a minibar and colour TV in every room.
I   Really? How many guestrooms are there?
R   There used to be forty-two rooms but we reduced it to thirty-eight because generally speaking, bedrooms in two-star hotels are not as spacious as in four-star hotels. We also needed to convert some of our small shower rooms to fully-equipped bathrooms.
I   What about the rest of the hotel? Did you have to make changes there too?
R   Oh yes, lots. The reception area has been made bigger and it is staffed twenty-four hours a day now. We also redesigned the bar and put in new sofas, armchairs, carpets and curtains.
I   It certainly looks very colourful. Do you employ more staff now?
R   Yes, we do, because we now provide a porter service, twenty-four-hour room service and a laundry service for guests. The other major change was to the food service. The standard of the cuisine's much higher now and we offer a wider range of food on our menu. But we still want the atmosphere to be as friendly as before, no matter how many stars we have!

Unit 6, Exercise 9 (CD Track 14)

One
A Excuse me, we're looking for the tennis courts.
B You need to go up a deck to the Lido deck and then it's at the front of the ship.
A That's great. Thanks.

Two
We would like to remind passengers that we are offering special discounts on many of our beauty treatments, including a free sauna and massage on selected deals.

Three
This is a passenger announcement. Please do not leave children unattended at the pools. Children under twelve must be accompanied by an adult.

Four
A Hello. I have an appointment at the hairdresser's at three o'clock but I can't find it.
B Don't worry, madam. It's just up these stairs and then first on your left.

Five
This is a public announcement. Tonight's film will start in fifteen minutes. Any passengers without tickets can buy them from reception on F deck. The film will begin at 7.30 pm.

Six
A I'm really hungry.
B So am I. What do you want to eat?
A I think there's an Italian restaurant next to the gym.
B OK. Let's go there.

Unit 6, Exercise 11 (CD Track 15)

1 It's very near.
2 They're going to Antigua.
3 You're not going to Capri.
4 I've been to Santorini.
5 She hasn't been there yet.
6 We've already been there.
7 He isn't going to the Seychelles.
8 We've been to Luxor and Karnak so far.

Unit 6, Exercise 13 (CD Track 16)

L The first thing to remember is that ideas about what makes a good curriculum vitae differ from country to country. In the UK it is generally accepted that a CV should be well presented on no more than one side of good-quality A4 paper. Your first objective is to sell yourself for the job you want.
S Excuse me, I have a question. What do you mean, 'sell yourself'?
L That's a good question. Well, I mean, you should think about the specific job on offer and include all the relevant experience you have in your CV. Don't use exactly the same CV for every job you apply for.
S I see. Thank you.
L Secondly, your CV should always be clear and easy to read. The third point is to make sure that your personal details, like name, address and telephone number, appear at the top of the document. Fourthly, put your qualifications and jobs in reverse chronological order so that the most recent appear first in the list. Finally, always remember to check your CV for spelling and grammatical mistakes. It's not going to impress an employer if you can't write correctly, is it?
S Should we write about our hobbies in the CV?
L That depends. Certainly emphasise your special abilities both in the workplace and outside, such as any languages you speak. Also mention any relevant hobbies such as team sports and voluntary work you do. This helps to give an idea of your personality. To conclude then, I want to remind you that the people who get interviews are not the ones with the best qualifications but those who write the best CVs!

Unit 7, Exercise 2 (CD Track 17)

B Good morning. How can I help you?
R Hi, we've booked a room.
B Could I have the name, please?
R Sure, it's Mr and Mrs Robert O'Donnell.
B Could you spell your surname for me, sir?
R O-apostrophe-D-O-N-N-E-L-L.
B Thank you, I'll just check on our computer. Yes, Mr O'Donnell, a double room for three nights. Would you mind showing me your passports, please?
R Our passports? Why do you need them?
B It's usual practice in South Africa, sir, to record the passport numbers of guests.
R Then I guess so. Leeta honey, where are the passports?
L Here Bob, I have them in my bag.
B Thank you. Would you like me to call your room when the passports are ready for collection?
R What? You want to keep them!
B It's just to save time now, sir. I can type the details into the computer later. Or do you mind waiting here now?
R Yes, I certainly do. We're tired after that flight and I need a shower and a rest.

B I understand, sir. Here's your key. You're in room two sixteen. Take the lift to the second floor and turn right. Would you like the porter to help you with your luggage?

L Yes, please. Now Bob, don't lift anything with your bad back.

B I'll call the porter for you. Breakfast is served from 8 am until 9.30 am. Check-out time is at twelve noon on the day of departure. Enjoy your stay and let us know if you need anything.

L Thank you, miss.

R But Leeta, I don't see why I can't carry the bags ...

Unit 7, Exercise 8 (CD Track 19)

R Hi Bev, got my passport?

B Yes, Mr O'Donnell. Here you are, sir.

R We were thinking of going shopping in the city centre for the afternoon. Is it safe?

B Yes, sir. You'll find that the centre of Cape Town is no different from other major cities. You must take a few precautions, though. If you're going shopping, I recommend that you use traveller's cheques or credit cards. You shouldn't take large amounts of cash. The markets are very crowded and lively but beware of pickpockets.

R Is that so? What about the camera?

B You should try not to attract attention to yourself by carrying cameras and wearing expensive jewellery.

L Sounds like we'd better leave our things in the safe deposit box in our room, honey.

R You're right, Leeta. We'll do that. Hey, now where did I put those car keys?

B If you are driving, sir, you must keep your car doors locked at all times.

R This is like being back home in Chicago!

B One last thing, avoid walking around the poorer areas of the city.

L How about going to see Robben Island?

B There are several ferries but it's best to book with an organised tour of the island. I can reserve your places for you here at the hotel. Oh, and another thing, it's a good idea to take a pill if you get seasick easily.

R Thanks Bev, you've been very helpful.

Unit 7, Exercise 14 (CD Track 20)

One

There were a lot of guests who wanted me to take their luggage. I told him I was busy and would come back in half an hour.

Two

I'm a receptionist, not a safari guide. Our usual guide was off sick, and the Hotel Manager said I needed experience in the bush. The animals frighten me.

Three

I gave him a photocopy with all the times and prices for our excursions. The thing is, the leaflet is from last year because we haven't had time to print the new one.

Four

He ordered one thing and then he changed his mind. The thing is, I'm the only waitress on night duty and we were fully booked that week.

Unit 8, Exercise 2 (CD Track 21)

M Good morning and welcome to *Holiday Options*. I'm Matt Scott and later today in the studio we have Lisa Barton – our very own tour operator. Lisa's going to tell us which resorts are going to be hot spots this summer. But first of all, we asked some of our listeners about their favourite holiday destinations.

LB So, what's your favourite holiday destination?

L1 My favourite place for a holiday? Corfu, Greece. We went there last year. It was great. Something for all the family.

L2 Oh, it's got to be Majorca. I love it – there's sun, sea and sangría. I've been to Majorca twice now and I'll definitely go again.

L3 I don't really have a favourite resort, but I'll probably go to the Mediterranean again, especially Turkey. The sightseeing's great. There's a fantastic place called, Pamukka ... Pamukkale. Yeah, and there are these incredible pools. It looks like snow, but it isn't.

Unit 8, Exercise 3 (CD Track 22)

M So, that's where some of our listeners are going, but what do you think, Lisa? Which holiday resorts are going to be the hot spots this summer?

L Well, a lot of people are going to Spain, Tenerife and, as we've just heard, the Balearic Islands. Also the Greek islands, like Corfu, are going to be popular.

M One of our listeners mentioned Turkey. Do you think Turkey'll be popular this year?

L I think it probably will, yes. You know, it's a great country. A real mix of East and West with some beautiful architecture and, of course, great beaches. And you don't get the crowds of tourists on the beaches as you do in, say, Spain.

M But there are lots of people in Bodrum!

L Yes, Bodrum is very popular, but there are other smaller places in the Mediterranean and inland that are more interesting.

M Tell us about Pamukkale, Lisa. It's one of Turkey's most famous tourist attractions, isn't it?

L That's right.

M And where does the name come from?

L The name Pamukkale means 'Cotton Castle' because it looks like it's made out of snow or cotton. It's because minerals in the water make the rock look white.

M Wow, it sounds incredible. So, can you swim in the water?

L I'm afraid not; the area is protected now by a UNESCO program. This means you can visit the hot springs, but you can't lie or swim in the pools. You can swim at any of the spa hotels though – they use water that comes directly from the springs.

M Sounds very relaxing. And do you think Turkey might be a hot spot for holidaymakers this year, then?

L It probably won't be as popular as Spain or Greece, but it may be one of the top ten destinations, yes.

M Thanks, Lisa. And if you'd like more information about holidays with a difference in Turkey and other destinations, you can visit our website on www.holidayoptions.com.

Unit 8, Exercise 4 (CD Track 23)

1 Good morning and welcome to *Holiday Options*.
2 Oh, it's got to be Majorca. I love it.
3 I've been to Majorca twice now.
4 Do you think Turkey'll be popular this year?
5 And do you think Turkey might be a hot spot?

Unit 8, Exercise 10 (CD Track 24)

One

As we know, people in western, industrialised countries generate most of the demand in the tourism industry. These people are now living longer and I believe this will affect the types of tourism people will want in the future. People will also probably take fewer long holidays, that is, a week or more, say, but instead short weekend breaks will become more popular because of changes in the way people work.

Two

It seems clear that travel times and costs will continue to come down and people will want to travel to more distant and exotic destinations in future. But the biggest change is the trend for more and more people to buy their holidays on the internet. New technology will even allow people to go on 'virtual tours' on their computers to see a holiday before they book it.

Three

With economic growth in countries like Russia, China, India, Indonesia and Thailand, there will be new tourists looking for holidays. What's more, we're likely to see more tourists travelling from eastern to western countries than in the past.

Four

I think that the number of 'new tourists' will increase in future. What I mean is someone who doesn't want mass-market tourism and wants more adventurous holidays. The majority of tourists will continue to buy package holidays, visit popular destinations and make their holiday choices based on the price, but increasingly the customer will expect more choice in how their package holiday is put togther.

Unit 8, Exercise 13 (CD Track 25)

Good morning, I'm Carlos Alvarez and I'm a member of the Hermosa Tourist Board. Today I'm going to talk about our proposal for a new resort on the island. First of all, I'd like to talk about how tourists will get to the island. Then I'll talk about the location of the new resort and its main attractions. Finally, I'll talk about accommodation.

First of all, how will visitors get to our island? In the past, the ferry was the only option. Well, now we plan to build a new airport to the south of Bellavista.

Secondly, the location. We have decided the best location for the resort is to the north of the ancient monuments. The main advantage of this is that the monuments are the most famous sight on the island and will attract the most tourists. A car park will be built near the stones. Yes, a car park, because of course a lot of buses and cars will need to park nearby. We are also going to build a visitors' centre with a museum, a shop and a restaurant and a café. That brings me to accommodation. Where are all these visitors going to stay? There will be three options on Hermosa: two hotels and a camp site. We're going to build two new hotels – a three-star hotel and a more luxurious hotel. Of course, I'm sure local people will continue to rent out rooms to visitors ...

To sum up, we think that the new resort by the monuments is the best option for both the people living on the island and its future visitors. It will be in the very centre of the island. It will be easily accessible by road and air and, more importantly, it will improve our island's economy and finally make Hermosa famous.

Unit 9, Exercise 8 (CD Track 26)

One

This is the last call for British Airways flight BA184, scheduled to depart at 18.35. Would Mr Hassan Razali please go to gate 45 immediately? The aircraft is ready to depart.

Two

American Airlines flight AA092 to London Heathrow is now boarding at gate 43.

Three

Can Mrs Henderson of Unibank please come to the information desk? Your driver is waiting for you.

Four

United Airlines flight UA906 scheduled to depart at 19.45 for London Heathrow has been cancelled. Passengers should contact the United Airlines desk for further information.

Five

British Airways flight BA188 to London Heathrow has been delayed and will now be departing at 21.20. Could passengers please go to gate 38.

Unit 9, Exercise 10 (CD Track 27)

I Tell me about your training to be cabin crew, David. What do you learn on the course?

D During the first two weeks training is basically about the airline and customer service. Things like how to read an airline ticket. We learn about the types of aircraft and their layouts. During those first two weeks you also collect your uniform and wear it for the first time. It's funny seeing all your colleagues in uniform for the first time!

I What happens next?

D The third and fourth weeks are the most intensive. It starts with general safety and emergency procedures and then you practise them on every type of aircraft. You're also taught all about the different safety equipment on board: lifejackets, fire extinguishers and so on.

I Do you do this on board the planes?

D No, in the training centre. You see, there are things called 'mockabs': they're the same size as real aircraft, and they have seats, galleys, doors, etc. – just like the real thing. You can even feel the movements of the aircraft when you are inside the mockabs. In the training sessions part of the group act as passengers and the rest as crew. The trainers then set up an unexpected situation and watch how the crew deal with the emergency. It is very important to learn all the procedures correctly; you need to know what to do.

I What kind of emergencies can you have?

D Emergencies can be an emergency landing or perhaps a fire. It feels very real. They even play the sounds of passengers screaming and engines running.

I That sounds really frightening. What else do you have to do?

D During these two weeks you also learn about aviation medicine: all types of medical emergencies from a little burn to helping a pregnant woman give birth.

I And what happens in the final week?

D Well, as long as you've passed your tests, you're taken onto a real aircraft in the final week. The aircraft visit is very important. It's when you discover how the real thing is. During the last week you also learn how to cook and deliver meals to the passengers, how to make drinks, and how to set up the drinks trolley. The next day is your first flight! Everybody is very excited. After that, the first six months are a probation period.

Unit 9, Exercise 12 (CD Track 28)

D Would you like any duty-free, madam?

P1 Oh yes, I'd like to buy some perfume. Do you have any l'Eau d'Issey?

D Yes, I think I do. I'll just get it for you. Here you are.

P1 How much is it?

D Let's see. It's the fifty millilitre bottle so that's twenty-nine pounds fifty, madam.

P1 Can I pay in dollars?

D Certainly, madam. But we only give change in pounds.

P1 Oh, that's OK.

D So that'll be forty-three dollars and thirty cents.

P2 Shall we get something for Barbara's daughter?

P1 That's a good idea. Do you have any soft toys?

D Yes, there are two. I've got a leopard and a teddy bear – he's called Wilbur.

P2 The leopard looks cute.

P1 It does, but I think I'll take the teddy bear.

D So that's forty-three thirty for the perfume plus fourteen dollars sixty for the teddy. That makes fifty-seven ninety.

P1 Here you are.
D Thank you.

Unit 10, Exercise 8 (CD Track 29)

L Excuse me, I've been attending the conference here and tomorrow I've got a free day to do some sightseeing. Do you have any information about the city?

R Yes, of course. What kind of information do you need exactly?

L You know, places to visit, but I haven't got much time because I'm flying back to the UK on Sunday night.

R Let me see. How about visiting the Wawel castle?

L Oh yes, my colleague said it's worth a visit.

R That's right. There's the castle, the cathedral and a cave. You must see the dragon's cave.

L And how long do you think it'll take to see everything?

R You'll probably need about three hours to see it all. Walking around the gardens takes some time.

L OK, that's a whole morning then.

R But, you should get there early because there are always very long queues.

L Oh, right. Oh, and one more thing. Are there any nice cafés or bars nearby?

R Well, the market square has lots of cafés and cellar bars. You know, bars underground.

L Really? Can you recommend one?

R Why don't you go to Pod Baranami?

L What's it like?

R It's famous for its cabarets. They also have a disco in the evenings.

L What time does the disco start?

R About 8 pm.

L I don't know, I don't really want to go dancing this evening.

R What about jazz? Do you like jazz?

L Oh, I love jazz.

R You could go to the pub, U Louisa. There's live jazz or blues music on Wednesdays.

L Sounds great. I think I'll go there in the evening. Thanks.

Unit 10, Exercise 11 (CD Track 30)

G Hello – excuse me – thank you. If I may have your attention please ... Thank you. Before we begin the tour, I'd like to give you a brief history of the castle. Wawel Hill was first inhabited by the Vistulan people in ancient times. Later, in the late medieval period, from the fourteenth century the royal residence and a new cathedral were built. But it was the kings of the Jagiellonian dynasty who turned this Gothic castle into one of the most magnificent Renaissance castles in Central Europe.

T Wasn't Cracow the capital of Poland?

G That's correct. Although Warsaw became the capital at the beginning of the seventeenth century, royal coronations continued to take place in Cracow and it remained a centre of historical and cultural importance.

T Wasn't it destroyed in the wars?

G Well, not exactly. In the seventeenth and eighteenth centuries the castle suffered from political conflicts, but an intensive restoration programme in the twentieth century saved the castle and cathedral. Fortunately, Wawel also escaped destruction in both world wars. Right, now let's turn to the statue of Tadeusz Kościuszko just in front of us. He was the general who was responsible for the insurrection of 1794 against the Russian army…

Unit 11, Exercise 3 (CD Track 31)

T What's the scenery like in New Zealand?

TO It's very varied. There are beaches, lakes, mountains, fjords and glaciers. I recommend you see Fox Glacier in Westland National Park, and Doubtful Sound, which is a fjord in the southwest. It's the deepest fjord in New Zealand. There's also an active volcano you can visit, Mount Ruapebu.

T That sounds interesting. What about the wildlife? Are there any dangerous animals, like kangaroos?

TO Not really, that's more Australia, but we have a lot of sheep here. There are forty-seven million sheep in New Zealand. There are more sheep than people.

T Really? Well, I think I'd like some information about tours to the fjords and glaciers, please.

TO Sure. Here's a map and a price list of excursions to the national parks. You can take a leaflet.

Unit 11, Exercise 5 (CD Track 32)

N Pacific Travel Company, Nathalie speaking. How can I help you?

S Hello, it's Stuart Gould here. I've booked a two-day group tour with your company and I need to make some changes to the original booking.

N Certainly, Mr Gould. Do you have your confirmation form with you?

S Yes, it's PTC ... PTC0189 dash 02.

N PTC0189 dash 02. That's a two-day Mount Cook

National Park Tour for a party of fourteen, departing on 23rd March. What changes would you like to make?

S   We'd prefer to go a day later, on 24th March. Is that possible? We're staying an extra day in Queenstown on the 23rd.

N   Just let me check Mr Gould. Yes, that's now confirmed. The coach leaves at 8.20 am from Newmans Terminal in Christchurch.

S   I'm sorry, could you repeat that, please?

N   Certainly, the coach leaves at 8.20 am from Newmans Terminal.

S   Thanks. And another thing, there are now only thirteen of us, so we'll need five double rooms and one triple room.

N   OK, Mr Gould, I'll make that change for you.

S   Also, can you tell me what time the bus returns to Christchurch?

N   The coach arrives back in Christchurch at approximately 6.15 pm.

S   Ah, you see we're flying to Auckland the following day to catch a connecting flight home to Scotland, so we're hoping to get a good night's sleep.

N   The coach service is generally very punctual, Mr Gould. I'm sure there'll be no problem.

S   Oh, good.

N   Now, I'll just confirm those changes. That's a group of thirteen, for the two-day Mount Cook National Park Tour, departing from Newmans Terminal at 8.20 am on Tuesday 24th March. The motel accommodation at Mount Cook is five double rooms and one triple room.

S   Yes, that's right.

N   I'll send you a fax today to confirm those changes, Mr Gould.

S   Goodbye and thank you very much for your help, Nathalie.

N   You're welcome. Goodbye Mr Gould.

Unit 11, Exercise 13 (CD Track 33)

One
TA Can I have your reservation number?
C1 Yes, let me see, it's – yes here it is, it's BGI oh two double seven.
TA Sorry, did you say B or V?
C1 It's B, B for Barcelona.

Two
TA Can you spell your surname for me, please?
C2 It's Doherty. That's D-O-H-E-R-T-Y.
TA Thank you, Miss Doherty.

Three
TA Sorry, I didn't catch that. Could you repeat your Visa card number?
C3 Yes, it's 3095 5541 8409 1057.
TA I'll just read that back to you. That's 3095 5541 8409 1057.
C3 That's right.
TA And the expiry date?

Four
C4 I'm phoning to confirm my booking.
TA Can I have your reference number, please?
C4 Yes, it's BED099415 dash 02.
TA Did you say D-E-B?
C4 No, BED099415 dash 02.
TA Thank you.

Five
C5 Have you got an email address?
TA Yes, we have. It's paradise at travelnet dot com.
C5 Is travelnet all one word?
TA Yes, it is.

Unit 12, Exercise 3 (CD Track 34)

One
Just a moment, sir. Here you are, size forty-three boots, your skis and poles. Now, when you're ready, go over there to that counter to have your bindings fitted correctly. Next?

Two
Put your pass into the machine this way up to open the gate and wait at the line for the chair to come round, then sit down when it touches the back of your knees and lower the safety bar. Be careful not to drop your poles.

Three
Now, to turn left you need to transfer your weight on to your right ski. Remember, your knees, hips and ankles must all work together. Watch me, like this. Ok, now you try it. Very good, Marisa.

Four
Just a few announcements. The coach will be outside the hotel every morning at half past eight to take you to the slopes. Anyone wishing to book lessons should speak to Jackie or myself. Finally, we've got a full programme of fun-packed entertainment in the hotel lounge every evening.

Five

This is the self-service food area, madam. We only serve sandwiches and drinks here. If you want a cooked meal, the restaurant is up the stairs on the first floor.

Unit 12, Exercise 15 (CD Track 36)

Good afternoon everybody. If I could just have your attention for one moment. I have some information for you about the activities we've organised for you this week with Inghams.

Thank you. We've lots of entertainment in store for you, starting this evening at half past eight with the welcome meeting in the hotel lounge.

You'll be delighted to know that includes a free drink. Now, tomorrow morning the ski school starts and then in the afternoon I'm leading a group cross-counrty skiing. Children aged twelve and over can come along, but they must be accompanied by an adult.

On Tuesday morning we'll be snowshoeing. In case you're not sure what that is, it's basically trekking in the snow wearing things that look like tennis rackets on your feet. But seriously, you don't have to be a skier to take part, we'll organise the hire equipment and it's lots of fun.

Now. Where was I? Oh yes, on Wednesday afternoon there's a demonstration of some fantastic new ski equipment in the hotel lobby.

Thursday evening at six o'clock there's a torchlit descent of the mountain. All you advanced skiers can participate in that if you want. We'll provide the transport from the hotel at 6 pm.

On Friday night we have our farewell party with a live band, dancing and there'll be a karaoke competition.

We'll also be organising lots of races and competitions throughout the week on the slopes and we're offering lots of super prizes.

You can sign up for the activities on the noticeboard in the hotel lobby and you can talk to me if you need any help or advice. I hope you all have a fantastic time this week with Inghams.

Unit 13, Exercise 11 (CD Track 37)

T So they're your travel details. Now, would you like to take out insurance through us? We have very competitive prices.

A What sort of insurance?

T Well, I'd recommend full health and travel insurance in your case, especially if you plan to go trekking in remote regions.

A I was thinking of going to my insurance company for that.

T We can provide a special package that meets your specific needs. You see, not all insurance includes high-risk activities like trekking and you might have to pay for any medical costs yourself. This insurance covers full costs for medical treatment, accidents and even evacuation by helicopter.

A Really? Let's hope I won't need that. Would this insurance pay my medical bills directly or refund me later?

T Let me see. It says here 'will cover your medical costs immediately'. The insurance also covers unexpected losses such as cancelled flights, stolen or lost cash, credit cards, passport or luggage. Let's see, you're going for twenty-one days – the cost is only seventeen dollars and fifty cents. It's well worth it.

A Yes, that does sound very reasonable. OK, I'll take it.

Unit 13, Exercise 15 (CD Track 38)

G OK everyone so we meet here tomorrow morning at 6.30. Please don't be late or we'll leave without you. Any questions?

T1 Yes, you see I've never been trekking before so I don't really know what to pack.

G My advice to you is to keep it simple. The less you have to carry the better. Don't take a big rucksack. Wear a good pair of trainers or lightweight trekking boots. Take two cotton T-shirts, two pairs of shorts and two pairs of socks.

T2 What about a towel?

G Yes, take a small towel or a sarong, which is even lighter. Pack a swimsuit for when we get to the waterfall. You'll also need toiletries, a simple medical kit, sun cream, a hat and sunglasses.

T1 Does it get cold at night?

G Yes, it does. We're in the winter season now so you'll need a sweater and long trousers or a tracksuit at night because it gets chilly. Also take a small torch because there is no electricity in the villages where we'll be staying. Oh, and don't forget your camera and extra film.

T1 Do we need waterproofs?

G No, it isn't the rainy season at the moment.

T2 Is there a danger of malaria in the region?

G Well, it's best to be careful and avoid mosquito bites as there might be a small risk. I recommend you use mosquito repellent at all times and wear long-sleeved shirts and long trousers at night. Right then, that's everything. I'll see you all tomorrow morning. Get a good night's sleep everyone, you'll need it.

Unit 14, Exercise 2 (CD Track 39)

R Are you checking out now, sir?

C Yes, that's right. Room four one seven.

R Here's your bill, Mr Collins. How would you like to pay?

C Hold on a minute, this can't be right. It says here 10,763 roubles. I think there's been a mistake. I've been overcharged.

R I'll just check that for you. The total includes room service which you ordered on the evening of the eighteenth. It was a chicken sandwich and a pot of coffee.

C Yes, that's right.

R This amount here is for the drinks you had from the minibar in your room.

C Yes, yes, but what's this 704 roubles for?

R That's the local government tax, which we have to charge. It's explained in the hotel information pack in your room.

C Well, what about this amount for phone calls? I don't remember making any phone calls.

R I'll just check our records. It says here that there was a call to the United Kingdom yesterday evening.

C Oh yes, that's right – I called my wife. But I was only on the phone for a couple of minutes – I can't believe it cost that much.

R We do have our own satellite dish here at the hotel, which adds to the cost. But I'll just check that for you. Oh yes, I do apologise, we have made a mistake here. This isn't the right amount, it should be 1,760 roubles, not 1,740. That makes a total of 10,783 roubles.

C But you can't charge me even more for that phone call!

R I'm sorry, sir. Would you like to pay by cash or credit card? I have to point out that there is a five percent surcharge if you want to pay by credit card.

C Oh no, it's already expensive enough. I'll pay by cash.

Unit 14, Exercise 12 (CD Track 40)

R Here's your bill, madam. Would you like to check it, please?

G That seems fine.

R Are you planning to visit St Petersburg again, madam?

G Actually yes, I am. I'm coming again in June for business.

R Just sign here, please. Thank you. Do you know there's a festival in June? The White Nights festival.

G Oh, what kind of a festival?

R Well, mainly classical music, but there's also opera, ballet and jazz concerts too. It's very well known. Guests usually book six months in advance. Here's your receipt.

G Thanks. Six months in advance?

R That's right, madam.

G I see. Well, I'll ask my PA to book a room when I get back to the office.

R If you like, I could book it for you now. It won't take a minute.

G Right. OK.

R Do you know when you're travelling?

G Let me check my diary. Yes, June 14th to 18th.

R So that's four nights, departing on the 18th?

G I'm not sure. Can I confirm later?

R Certainly. I'll just check availability. Oh good, we still have our mini-suites. For only twenty dollars more, I can book you a mini-suite. I'm sure you'll find it more comfortable for meetings.

G Mmm, only twenty dollars. OK, I'll ask my PA to confirm it with you. By the way, what will the weather be like?

R Oh, it can be quite sunny, that's why it's the best time of year for a festival. It never gets dark.

G Really? And will I have to book tickets in advance?

R Yes, but that's no problem. Here's a programme. You can fax me and our concierge will be happy to book them for you.

G Oh, right. That's great. Thanks for everything.

R Not at all. We look forward to seeing you in June, Ms Reed.

Unit 15, Exercise 6 (CD Track 42)

This is the weather forecast for Mexico today, Tuesday September 20th. There have been heavy storms in Mexico City this week and these are expected to continue today. Temperatures will be up to 73 degrees during the day, falling to around 56 at night. Moving to the north of the country, it will be overcast in Chihuahua but temperatures are high, rising to 90 degrees during the day. In the centre of the country temperatures are not expected to be as high. In Guadalajara it will get up to 79 degrees and there will be lots of heavy rain. The level of humidity will be around 97 per cent. On the south coast it will also be extremely hot, humid and wet. There will be heavy rain in Acapulco and the average daytime temperature will be around 90 degrees, with humidity reaching 94 percent. Moving on to Mérida in the Yucatán Peninsula, expect lots of sunshine and high temperatures. The daytime high will be around 91 degrees with a humidity level of 85 percent. The sunshine will continue for a few days but satellite pictures show rain and strong winds are due to reach the region later in the week. And that's all from the weather desk.

Unit 15, Exercise 8 (CD Track 43)
One

Its coastal influences and variations in altitude make Mexico a country of great contrasts. The north is the Mexico of popular imagination and cowboy films with its great mountains, deserts, canyons, arid plains and giant cacti. In fact, over half of Mexico's land has very little rainfall each year. Mexico is a land of mountains with more than half the country over one thousand metres. In the south, the tropical plains of the Gulf Coast are very green and fertile and there are spectacular rainforests on the Atlantic coast.

Two

There is something very special about the Mayan culture and the beauty of their great stone cities and pyramids in the jungle. We also know that they had a very advanced knowledge of astronomy. They observed and predicted the phases of the moon and solar and lunar eclipses. Archaeologists have studied the sites of the Mayan civilisation for many years but today there still remains the mystery of their sudden decline and disappearance before the arrival of the Spanish conquistadors in the sixteenth century.

Three

Mexico received over twenty million tourists last year and over eighty percent of these visitors were from the United States. The country is the seventh most popular tourist destination in the world. What's more, the tourism industry is second only to the oil industry in Mexico and is growing very quickly. The government and business communities recognise the importance of tourism for the country's future development and there are major plans for expansion of the industry. In the next ten years the number of hotel rooms will increase by twenty percent. There will also be improvements to airports, public transportation, restaurants and recreational facilities.

Unit 15, Exercise 13 (CD Track 44)
One

I come down to Mexico City about once a month on business. I usually stay a few nights at one of the chain hotels – Fiesta Americana is very reliable, and the Hotel Real has a nice pool with jacuzzi. If you travel as much as I do, you need a hotel where you can relax. Mexican food? Oh, I love Tex-mex. It's hot and spicy. The only thing is, the service isn't as good as it is in California. I don't get much time for sightseeing but when I have an hour or so, I love going shopping in the markets. They sell a lot of Indian arts and crafts so I sometimes buy ceramics or rugs for my family back home.

Two

We did the Mayan route a few years ago. We went to Guatemala and southern Mexico. We saw lots of Mayan ruins, but the best ones were in Palenque, which is in the jungle. It was great, but really hot and humid. We had to be careful because the steps on the pyramid weren't very wide and you could fall – they weren't like the big stones in the pyramids in Egypt. Oh, and we made sure we had a good first aid kit. Even though we used lots of insect repellent we were still bitten by mosquitoes.

Three

We usually go somewhere in Spain or maybe to some European city for a long weekend. But we thought we'd like to go somewhere more exotic for our honeymoon. It's only once in a lifetime, isn't it? So, we've booked a four-star hotel on Isla Mujeres, which is a tiny island just opposite Cancún. I didn't want to stay in Cancún because people say it's very crowded. Anyway, we're flying from Madrid two days after the wedding and we're staying for ten nights. Juan says he's just going to relax on the beach after all the stress of the wedding but I'm definitely going to do some snorkelling and scuba diving – they say the coral and the fish are amazing!

English for International Tourism features material taken from DK's acclaimed
Eyewitness Travel Guide Series

Over 70 titles covering key destinations. Whether for Florida or France, Cracow or California,
Sydney or Singapore, you're as good as there with DK Eyewitness Travel Guides.

www.dk.com